FROM ANSCHLUSS TO ALBION
Memoirs of a refugee girl
1938-1940

Elisabeth M Orsten

Acorn Editions
Cambridge

Acorn Editions
P. O. Box 60
Cambridge
CB1 2NT

British Library Cataloguing in Publication Data:
A catalogue record is available from the British Library

ISBN 0 9065 5417 9

Printed by Biddles Ltd,
Guildford & Kings Lynn

CONTENTS

PREFACE

Hitler's invasion of Austria took place in March 1938, four months after my tenth birthday. After some delay, I was finally evacuated to England and spent almost two full years there, separated from my own family. Despite not knowing a word of the language before I arrived, I quickly put down roots in English soil, and was deeply unhappy at having to pull these up again in order to be reunited with my parents in yet another place of refuge. This story describes the impact which that first new language and culture had on me. Why am I writing it? Primarily for myself of course, but also because it may help to explain how a child feels when snatched out of its world and suddenly placed into another. Children do not easily express their feelings, especially when these are as complicated and ambiguous as is the trauma of adjustment to a new environment. A child that is torn between two countries and confronted by divided loyalties, perhaps even afraid of further displacement, in what stranger can it trust, to whom would it dare to complain?

While today there are thousands of such children, many of whom have been displaced under far harder conditions than I ever experienced, nevertheless, we share something in common. In my Austrian childhood, the young were simply told what to do and barred from all knowledge of what went on in the real world of the adults. Though today's refugee children know a great deal more about their war-torn universe, they too are accustomed to lack of power and to the experience of having to live in a world which does not always appear to make much sense. For the sake of these children then, and for the adults trying to care for them, what I am recounting here may provide some insights. As a refugee child, I too was frequently unable to express my true feelings, and sometimes did not dare to do so, even though my host family was anxious to help me. Plucked out of this first haven of refuge after such a relatively short time could easily have blotted out all my experiences there, had not a life-long affection for England, and repeated visits as an adult, kept those distant memories alive. The latter are sometimes re enforced, and sometimes contradicted, by my German-English diary which I am now, some fifty-odd years later, rereading for the first time. The book itself was a goodbye gift which was especially dear to me, and hence I tried to write in it fairly regularly – something that I have never managed to do since. Yet how reliable are these entries which, though certainly naïve, are often quite self-conscious? For that matter, how reliable is my memory now that there is no one left to verify or deny particular events? Thus forced to sift between two sources, both of them slightly suspect, these pages can only hope to arrive at some approximation of the truth. Even so, this truth deserves to be told.

CHAPTER I
CHILDHOOD JOYS AND FEARS

Perhaps somewhere in the world there still exists that little silver engraved cross which my father gave me at the Westbahnhof in Vienna one bleak January morning. It must have been inexpensive because otherwise it would have been confiscated by the Nazis at the border. The following day I arrived in England, wearing my father's parting gift and clutching a large celluloid doll with movable limbs, called Trude. Only much later, as an adult did I learn from my English foster-mother that when she came to Bloomsbury House expecting to collect an eleven-year old girl, she saw Trude before becoming aware of me and said to herself with considerable surprise "But I thought that the child would be bigger!" Generously, Mrs. C. had been prepared to accept me into her home for an indefinite period, but less than two years later I had to be evacuated once more, this time across the U-boat infested Atlantic. As far as I can remember, the little silver cross was still around my neck, and the big doll accompanied me as well, safely wrapped in a package. In the New World, however, circumstances forced me to be far more grown-up than I really was, and consequently poor Trude disappeared without a trace shortly after my arrival there. So, at some indeterminate moment, did the little cross. Both these objects are intimately connected with my childhood stay in England, as well as with some of its difficulties. But before describing that time, it is necessary to go back to the beginning. , , ,

Yet where does one start? Surely not with 11 March 1938, when Hitler, testing the international waters, first invaded Austria. Too many other events need to be accounted for which made that successful rape possible! Similarly, too much in my own life had already shaped me by then, making me both uniquely vulnerable as well as resilient to what was about to engulf us all. The notion of a simple, idyllic childhood, suddenly destroyed by invading forces, is a picture painted by adults for propaganda purposes.

On the surface, of course, my childhood was not a particularly troubled one. Born into the comfortable middle class of reasonable wealth and professional standing, I knew nothing of the poverty and social unrest which seemed to be a legacy of the First World War and the dismemberment of the Austro-Hungarian Empire. I am told that one day, aged between two and three, I was found gazing with some interest into a mirror. When asked what I was looking at, I replied, "A Pwincess". To the query, "And what is the Princess called?", I responded with my own name. Even though I do not remember this event, that particular term of endearment undoubtedly came from my father, who was lovingly proud of me, his first-born. Unfortunately I could not see a great deal of him, since he was a devoted, able, and highly conscientious physician, who was extremely busy, running a large private clinic or sanatorium. This institution enjoyed a high reputation, particularly as regards the treatment of heart diseases, and patients came to it from all over the world. On rare occasions, my younger brother and I were allowed to visit my father's hospital chambers, and many patients expressed their gratitude by sending something from their homeland for us children. Sometimes we received unexpected toys, but more usually the gift took the form of fine linen or lace or perhaps an exquisitely embroidered garment from India. Such display, however, was meant for adult admiration, and reserved for special occasions. Children put on what they were told to put on, and had no say in the matter. Generally we were suitably and simply dressed. When needed, new materials and patterns would be selected by my mother or by some close relative, and Frau Wolff, a faithful family retainer who had already sewn dresses for my mother when she was young, would come to us for the required length of time. After several painstaking fittings, I would have to show off the finished product for the satisfaction of my mother as well as for the approval of whoever had presented me with the new garment. I myself was not expected to have any opinion or preference, and if someone remembered to ask "Don't you like your nice new dress?", the question was merely rhetorical. No doubt my clothes were carefully chosen, but the only outfit which I remember with distinct pleasure is a smart orange skating costume which my mother knitted for me. To the skirt and top she added a little fur muff as well as a hat trimmed with a border of that selfsame fur, made from an old coat which she had discarded. Wearing this costume bolstered my morale and helped to make me more proficient on the ice. However by then my days in Vienna were already drawing to a close, and so I am getting a little ahead of myself.

The first years of my life passed peacefully enough although, like most infants, I have no clear recollection of them. Little except obedience was expected of me, and the nursemaids who looked after me were young and kind. When I was not quite three, my brother was born, and my earliest memories are linked with him. There is the occasion when, in an effort to toilet-train him, he was tied to his potty. Frustrated, he is pulling himself along in our room, furiously banging his head on the floor and turning beet-red. There is a slightly later occasion when, still a toddler, he is sick, but clamours to have his favourite green outfit hung over the railings of his bed. Talented and strong-willed, he had a violent temper, inherited from my mother, and since he was also an extremely attractive child, with huge black eyes, fringed with long lashes, as well as a button nose and mouth, he probably got his way more often than was good for him. Both of us were looked after by a nanny who was known to the whole family as Fräuli, a form of address clearly combining respect and affection, since this name is the diminutive form of the German word for "Miss", and could be translated as "Missy". In my generation, there were countless middle-class children who depended on such a figure, who was their own special "Fräuli". Our Fräuli was my mother's age and came of wealthy peasant stock. Before 1914, unfortunately, the family had lost most of its holdings, including a very profitable inn, and so the many siblings had dispersed to seek their living elsewhere. How Fräuli first came to us I do not know, but she seems to have been adopted into our home before my brother was born, because my father arranged to have her take a special course in infant care to prepare for the event. She was an intelligent woman, kind but firm, who had had little opportunity for formal education. Later on, when I was going to school, she watched over my homework; the fact that she was picking up correct spelling and grammar from me, was something of which I was not aware. Deeply attached to her childhood home, about which she told us many stories, at heart she remained connected to her peasant culture. On summer afternoons when we explored the cool, mysterious woods with her, she would show us how to weave baskets out of fir branches, filled with soft moss and with tiny flowers. On the other hand, she also warned us never to eat a banana whose skin contained black spots since this would bring on leprosy, nor to eat our food standing up because this would cause it to go down into our legs and make them inordinately heavy – advice which for years we firmly believed!

Fräuli quickly became my shield and my refuge. For, as I reached school age, I grew increasingly introspective and timid; any unexpected or new experience terrified me. Exactly how and why this process started is beyond my recall today, but possibly some childhood illness – for I was prone to a great many – set it off. Undoubtedly, competition with my aggressive little brother also played a role, along with the fact that as I grew older, more was expected of me, and I was always afraid of not meeting adult expectations. Often I was so frightened that I could not eat, and being made to do so, with a spoon being literally pushed into my mouth, only made matters worse. If Fräuli was there, then the atmosphere was more relaxed, and I could cope. In my mother's presence I became paralysed.

The youngest of three daughters, and born into an extremely wealthy family, whose circumstances had been somewhat reduced by the Great War, my mother was pretty, graceful and athletic. Early in life, however, a somewhat prickly temperament had earned her the nickname of "Little Hedgehog". Having suffered from a severe and repressed Victorian upbringing, she wanted to spare her children a similar ordeal, but lacked maternal warmth and had no patience with childish failings. Probably I only received a light slap in the face once or twice, but this sufficed to make me flinch whenever her temper rose. Not introspective by nature and limited in her self-awareness, my mother seldom realised how her words and actions might affect me. Thus, when I was about nine or ten, she showed me a string of genuine pearls, saying that they were mine to wear when I was grown up and that for the time being I had to look after them. This strange present made little impression on me – particularly since my mother had not chosen a special occasion for its presentation – but nevertheless I put it carefully away. Then one dreadful evening, when I looked into the box where the pearls were supposed to be, they had disappeared. Obviously this was somehow my fault! Over the next few days, despite the terrible lump in the pit of my stomach, I did not dare tell anyone what had happened! Eventually my mother casually mentioned that she had decided to take the pearls back again because I was really too young to look after them, and with a great deal of relief, I forgot all about the matter. Only now do I understand that my poor mother, whose puritanical upbringing did not allow for the slightest piece of finery – even in old age she still recalled with great bitterness a small bracelet which had been taken away from her and handed over to another child – was attempting to let her small daughter enjoy what she herself had been denied in her youth.

Unlike my mother, I was not athletically inclined. On weekend outings, struggling up the hills of the Vienna Woods, I was always far behind everyone else, calling out a despairing "Wait for meeee". Gym was the subject which caused me the most trouble at school, for climbing ropes or turning cartwheels was quite beyond me. Although I enjoyed ice-skating in one of the many small local outdoor rinks, it took me a long time to build up any kind of confidence; in fact, I was encouraged to pursue this activity mainly in the hope of strengthening my weak ankles. Eventually I became an enthusiastic swimmer, the only sport at which I ever excelled, but this was not so at the beginning. One autumn day in my second year of primary school, we were taken to a public pool and allowed to paddle around as we pleased, while those who could swim were encouraged to leave the shallow water. Although I had already been taught the rudiments of swimming the previous summer, I remained among the non-swimmers, for the deep end seemed very threatening. After school, in reply to my mother's probings, I admitted the truth, for as a child I never lied – I was much too afraid of being found out! Angered by my cowardice, she would not speak to me for several days. Her reaction to my failure was caused in part by maternal solicitude, since she did not want me to grow up suffering from her own fear of water. Equally strong, however, was her maternal pride which demanded visible achievements. Unhappily, I only sensed the latter.

Thus, fear of my mother permeated much of my childhood. If Fräuli was aware of this, her urgings to be "good" and to please my parents did little to help, though her mere presence was some check on my mother's outbursts. In Vienna, we all lived in close quarters, which clearly exacerbated problems. In the late twenties and early thirties, the city was still suffering a housing shortage, and suitable flats were difficult to find and expensive to buy. My father had done his best, but it was a long way from the grandeur and the spaciousness in which my maternal grandparents still lived. Visiting them in the elegant Third District was always a delight. There were cosy studies and sitting-rooms where I would read with them, or be read to, and lofty dining and drawing-rooms which I could explore at will. The latter contained a sculptured figure – which I presumed to be an angel although it lacked both clothing and wings – standing on the floor near the concert grand. Going into the room alone, I would crouch down and stroke the marble back and flanks, feeling their cool roundness. While my grand-father introduced me early to great German literature, particularly to heroic poetry which I quickly memorised and loved to declaim, my grandmother preferred moral stories. As their only

grand-children, we were always indulged, and chocolate, normally
a rare treat, usually appeared before the visit was over.

If my grandparents' Viennese flat provided a contrast to our
own cramped quarters, even more space and freedom were available
in the summer when we went to stay at our paternal family home,
located in the Carinthian resort town where my father had been
born. Since neither his parents nor his younger sister were still
living, we were the only family visitors. At the time, I was so
surrounded by uncles and aunts, great-aunts and grand-parents,
not to mention distant cousins, on my mother's side, that I never
wondered about the other half of my parentage. My father's father,
a military physician, had married so late in life that on a photo
which shows him in uniform, holding his son and daughter, he
looks more like their grandfather. Not surprisingly, he had died
long before my mother and father became engaged. Early in their
marriage, he and his wife had moved to Austria from Hungary, and
had cut all ties with their former homeland and all their relations
there. Much later, my mother told me that Omama, my paternal
grandmother, refused to ever speak about them. Hence whatever kith
and kin existed on my father's side were irretrievably lost.

Omama lived in Vienna and died there when I was about six.
My memory retains only a comfortable, heavy-set figure, who
would visit us children, bringing along her cancelled tram ticket.
Pushing chairs together, we would then pretend that we were riding
a tram. However she played such a small role in our lives that her
death made no impression on me; possibly I was not even told
about it. Of more significance to me was the death of my father's
sister which had occurred before I was born. Mitzi was supposed
to have been a stunningly beautiful girl, but wilful and giddy,
who loved to dance all night. She married an extremely wealthy
man who doted on her and even hired a private train to take her to
Switzerland when she became ill with tuberculosis. According to
Fräuli, nevertheless poor Mitzi refused to give up parties and
dancing, and so she died on her return from Switzerland. Since I
was said to resemble my father's sister, no doubt the story was
meant as a warning!

The former family home was let for most of the year, with a
tiny cottage in the garden for the couple who looked after the
property. Their duties included despatching the crop of peaches
which had ripened late against the white stucco walls of the house.
Each autumn, a crate would arrive in Vienna, carefully packed,
and carrying with it memories of a blissful summer. The warm

and tranquil water of the large lake, the family hotels near the beach, a muscular, Teutonic swimming instructor whom one could engage for private lessons, all these combined to make Velden a popular summer resort for middle class children. Some amusing photos in the family album show that I was already taken there by my mother when I was a toddler. Later on, my brother and I made the long train journey accompanied by Fräuli, in whose care we spent the two months' holiday. My father would join us for as long as he could get away, but part of his vacation had to be devoted exclusively to my mother who always preferred skiing or mountain climbing in the Alps.

Although I learnt to swim fairly quickly when I was about five years old, it took considerably more effort to persuade me to trust the watery element without any external aid. Eventually rather drastic methods were used. One afternoon, while my mother was there to supervise the process, all of us went out in a rowboat, accompanied by my swimming instructor. When we were some distance from the shore, I was told to jump into the water, but given my usual timidity, naturally didn't dare to do so. Thereupon the instructor simply threw me overboard! Though such an approach might have backfired, and undoubtedly would not be used today, in my case it achieved the desired end. Since I was already a good swimmer, initial shock was followed by the realisation that I could cope, and with this awareness of my own abilities came the pleasure of striking out towards a boundless, wide horizon. After that there was no holding me back – during the holidays the bookworm turned into a water rat!

Besides the enjoyment of swimming, which formed a special bond between my father and myself, the summer offered other pleasures. Our midday meals were often eaten in a particular hotel dining-room which seemed deliciously cool after hopping across the hot beach sand with bare feet, carrying one's shoes. Intriguingly, instead of initials as on our own sets at home, each piece of the massive cutlery here bore the inscription "Stolen from Hotel M". Supper was a simple meal at home. As special treat we indulged in corn on the cob, purchased earlier that day from the gypsies who went from door to door with pack loads of sweet corn, offering to mend kettles and to sharpen knives and scissors. Everyone considered them a bad lot, liable to steal anything that they could lay their hands on, especially small children, but since Fräuli was always with us, we were never afraid of them. From time to time, bands of musicians, including the famous Russian Cossack Choir, would give an afternoon concert. Every week, using a sail-boat which slowly covered the shoreline of the lake, one of the hotels widely advertised special evening dances, many of which were meant for children. Though we never attended any such public entertainments, today I can still recall white sails with huge orange-red letters, boldly displaying the name of the Hotel B. and hear once more the stentorian announcement coming through a hand-held megaphone, slowly growing more faint as the boat passed along to the next little resort. On rare occasions, we might glimpse fairy lights across the lake. Once every summer, to the delight of small boys, the town's fire-fighting equipment was tested and displayed to the summer guests, and one or two daring local lads showed off on an improvised slide.

By the end of August, we travelled back to Vienna. Leaving Velden was always sad, but the journey itself was exciting. Above all, we were fascinated by the hypnotic rhythm of the train, a kind of "dadā dadā" which might become slower or faster, depending on the speed with which the wheels turned. My brother and I loved this sound, and later that night we would beat it out on our pillows. Whenever the train chugged through tunnels or around curves, it gave a warning whistle as if the engine were finding the work very hard – this was even better than the various train sets my brother had at home, with which we both played! Travelling back to Vienna, we always seemed to have a spacious compartment to ourselves, with plenty of room for our playthings, while over our heads there were deep, strong nets to hold all the luggage. When my brother was quite small and had become tired and restive, Fräuli used to put him up there, where he went peacefully to sleep, while I felt very superior and grown-up.

The conclusion of the holidays meant a return to school, which I enjoyed but also dreaded, though nothing ever occurred there that should have caused such fear. However, school represented authority, and I associated all principal authority with my mother. (Fräuli's authority was a delegated one.) Therefore breakfast often stuck in my gullet, and frequently came up again. This pattern started when, two months short of my sixth birthday, I entered the first form in our local primary school. Here work was already taken very seriously, unlike the private French kindergarten to which I had been sent earlier. The reason for this was that, unless they were being educated in a private convent school, *all* children, regardless of economic background, attended the first four years of primary school in common. Since those from the poorer homes often would only get very limited schooling, it was important for them to receive solid grounding as quickly as possible. Following this shared experience, middle class children had to pass an examination to enter the fee-paying *Gymnasium*, one for boys, and one for girls, while poorer children attended a public high school which was less geared to purely academic subjects and which they could leave early to go to work. Since I was a frail and high-strung youngster, various illnesses made me miss almost sixty days in the first year of school, and over ninety in the second. At various periods, I had to be excused from certain activities, like gym and close needle work, and since I was not particularly adept at either, I did not mind this at all. As far as the strictly academic curriculum was concerned, however, thanks to a few weeks of private coaching I was always able to keep up with the assigned work, and moved from one form to the next in the normal way. Primary school taught all the basics, with a great deal of emphasis on our handwriting, because we had to master first the spiky German script, and then the cursive hand of the Roman alphabet. Teachers were demanding but kind. Looking at my school reports now, where my overall standing was excellent, I am convinced that they gave me far better marks in singing, gym and drawing than I deserved, simply because they did not wish to spoil my record. When halfway through my first year of school one place in the classroom became vacant, our form mistress announced, half-jokingly, that because I was such a good girl, I could have that seat as well as my own. This was a most unwelcome gift. My normal place was next to a friend from my own social background, while the spare seat was beside one of the poorer girls whom I did not know. Fearing that this child would feel slighted and not wishing to hurt her feelings, I hastily whispered an explanation to my friend, and then moved to sit beside my new neighbour. My action was purely instinctive, but in retrospect, I rather doubt that the other girl welcomed it; she certainly was not particularly friendly. By a curious coincidence, one of my mother's sisters, already a rabid socialist in her teens, had behaved similarly when, in protest against class distinctions, she had insisted on eating in the kitchen with the servants, undoubtedly cramping their style by her presence – a story family friends only told me years later.

Traditionally, Austria was a Catholic country, and therefore all state-run schools subscribed to that faith. Before and after our morning and afternoon classes, there were prayers, led by the classroom mistress. In the first year, she also gave us basic religious instruction. From the second year on, a young chaplain came once a week, thus making religion a distinct and important subject which non-Catholics did not attend. In the first form, however, such instruction was merely part of our daily curriculum, like spelling and arithmetic. While I am not aware of early discrimination on religious grounds, and the school respected freedom of conscience, it was easy to know to which denomination you belonged. During daily prayers, all of us stood as a sign of respect. Jewish children, however, remained silent throughout, and Protestants only joined in the Lord's Prayer, while Catholics continued with the Hail Mary and finished with the Doxology. When at the start of school, I joined in this recitation, our classroom mistress suggested that my parents might object to this practice, since I was officially registered as belonging to no religious affiliation. Yet though I too had to be silent throughout and was not allowed to join in the prayers, I absorbed a certain amount of religious instruction from the classroom, as well as from the culture all around me. In the second form, I was officially enrolled as a Catholic and thus could share fully all aspects of school life. That story, however, belongs to the next chapter – here I am dealing primarily with events connected with my earliest education.

Although I cannot clearly recall any time when books were not part of my life, at first someone must have been reading them to me, because whatever I might have picked up before, officially, children learned to read in their first year of schooling. The logical and consistent manner in which German sounds and letters connect made this process very easy, and by Christmas I was reading fluently. No doubt we were given fairly elementary books in school, though I cannot remember any of these. At home I turned very soon to history and legend, and for many years my favourite reading remained a somewhat simplified version of Homer's *Iliad*. I wept over the destruction of Troy, loved the brave Hector, and detested the wily Odysseus because trickery had no place in my heroic universe. Greek legends were soon followed by the Norse ones, almost as interesting but more difficult to understand because they depicted less clear-cut values or obvious heroes. Among fairy tales, which definitely occupied a much lower place, I preferred those of Hans Christian Andersen, and had no use for the Brothers Grimm or for Aesop's *Fables* which seemed to me to be preaching a utilitarian morality and to be ignoring loftier ideals; but of course I kept this opinion to myself. Soon early Germanic history also became exciting, particularly when it dealt with figures from the

Nibelungenlied. Wisely, my parents tried to balance all this literary material with interesting books designed to teach me a little about natural history and science.

While much of my reading was prose, I really preferred poetry and was encouraged in this by my grandfather with whom I started at an early age reading Schiller's dramatic poems dealing with heroic classical themes. Rhyme was in any case very much part of my Germanic culture. Through school we became familiar with many pithy aphorisms, expressed in couplet form, all rather like "You must not unto another do/ What you don't want him to do to you". Every summer, we got amusing letters and postcards from my grandfather, written in verse, and even my parents could express themselves in this vein, if they felt like it. Early in life, my first ambition had been to become a Greek goddess, so that I could right the wrongs of Troy. When I realised that this was impossible, I determined to become the greatest and most famous poet ever, in whose epic work the Trojans would overcome the Greeks. Soon I was experimenting with verse forms, but these first attempts, like my early ambitions, remained my secret. Meanwhile at school, we started writing little prose compositions which I found far less exciting. We were encouraged to practise even over the holidays, since we were expected to keep a diary during the summer, to be shown to our form mistress when we returned in September. Not surprisingly, once memories of the classroom had faded, this tiresome task was neglected, until the day for our departure from Velden drew near, when I would hastily begin to fill in my blank entries, pestering Fräuli for details of what we had done on any particular day; invention at the expense of truthfulness never occurred to me.

Even though the books I read at home provided wider horizons than those prescribed by the school curriculum, neither one dealt with the problems of my own country, let alone with its relationship to the rest of Europe. Geography is not listed on my primary school report cards while in place of world history, we studied a subject called "*Heimatkunde*" (Study of one's Native Land), which delved far back into the legendary past of Austria, and taught us about her provinces, rivers and mountains, but carefully avoided anything controversial. We learnt numerous military songs, including the well known march *Ich hatt' einen Kameraden*, glorifying a faithful, fallen comrade, and the rather melancholy *Morgenrot*, in which a young soldier laments that with the coming of dawn the sun will rise on his untimely death.

That these verses were connected with any recent historical events was beyond our understanding. Most popular of all was a rather lugubrious patriotic song about the great Tyrolean martyr, Andreas Hofer, which celebrated Andreas' love of his homeland and his heroic stance facing the firing squad at Mantua. No one told us how these historical occurrences had come about, nor that they reflected badly on the Hapsburg dynasty. For during the Napoleonic wars, Andreas, an simple citizen of Innsbruck but a born leader, had successfully defended the Tyrolean region against the French and the Bavarians. Though at first the Austrian Emperor had encouraged this patriotic stand, political expediency had caused him to cede Tyrol to the Bavarians, abandoning Andreas to capture and execution. So in the classroom we glorified heroism and death in battle, understanding little, but suspecting that at its heart, life was filled with sadness and terror. Indeed, such an attitude had already been inculcated in us earlier by various popular rhymes meant for small children. While English toddlers were riding to Banbury Cross to see a fine lady make joyful music with her jingling jewellery, we had been bounced on someone's knee to verses which told us about a hapless rider who couldn't help crying out when he fell off his horse because ravens were waiting to devour him, should he land in the ditch. Similarly, a lullaby which my mother frequently sang, accompanying herself on the piano, urged the little one to sleep securely, even though outside the rain was falling and the neighbour's barking dog was snapping at a beggar and tearing his pitiful rags. In that kind of world, a trumpet call to battle and a young soldier dying at dawn seemed fitting subjects for school songs, though who was fighting whom and why, no one tried to explain.

Given such a limited approach to history, it was not surprising that current affairs played no role at all in the curriculum. Nor was this void filled at home. However, at least we knew that there had been something called the First World War, and could connect the event with our parents. My mother, a schoolgirl in her late teens at the time, had got into terrible trouble once in her Geography class because when she had been asked to locate France, pointing to the map, she had jokingly said, "France: Up, Austria: Down". My father, while still a medical student, had served in the Imperial Army, where he had learnt to ask the wounded in a number of languages, "Where does it hurt?" He also seemed to know rather different words to a song which we had been taught at school, in which we were exhorted to be loyal and honest at all times; in my father's military version, the promised reward for such faithfulness was very peculiar and did not make sense to us. Nor did these few details fit together to make any coherent whole of what had happened before we were born. Occasionally, sharp little ears might catch some snide criticism of Austrian politics, but even if, for instance, one had heard Dollfuss called "an idiot", what was one to make of that? Our childhood world contained no news media of any kind. I can vaguely remember a crystal radio set, though we were probably not allowed to touch it without the presence of an adult, and anyhow, it was difficult to make out any coherent speech through all that static. Newspapers belonged in coffee-houses, where they were put on special frames so that grown-ups could read them comfortably over their coffee; if any papers ever came into the house, they were definitely not meant for children. Television still lay in the future. Hence we knew nothing about the various world crises which were brewing all around us in the thirties. I could indulge my imagination as much as I liked on the epic Trojan battles, totally unaware of the real wars going on in Spain and in Abyssinia, as Ethiopia was then called; I was equally ignorant about events close at hand. Only a hint of the bitter battles fought in the streets of Vienna in 1934 ever reached me at the special clinic where I was recuperating after a lengthy illness during my second year of primary school. The clinic was situated at some distance outside the city, and one afternoon during our usual rest period on a covered veranda, we children heard faint gunfire, coming from the direction of the capital, but none of the staff told us anything, or even admitted that something unusual was happening. When at last I was able to return to the classroom, I discovered that we were learning a new song which exhorted us to close ranks behind a dead leader (*Ihr Jungen schliesst die Reihen gut, Ein Toder führt Euch an*), and proclaimed that Chancellor Dollfuss had shed his blood for Austria; the fatal bullet had awakened his people, so that now a new day was dawning for us all. Obviously something dreadful had taken place while I was away. However, nobody offered to explain what had actually happened, or why, and it did not occur to me to ask. What went on in the adult world was not supposed to be our concern. Obedient middle-class children did not question this limitation of their horizons, accepting it as perfectly natural and right. Besides, school, homework and private lessons already took up so much precious time that I was glad to be left to my reading and daydreaming.

CHAPTER II
MIXED MESSAGES

Outwardly then, the years were tranquil and followed a regular pattern, especially after I had outgrown most of my childhood illnesses. Spring came early, for by the beginning of February the first snowdrops could already be found in the Vienna Woods, growing between the last snow crusts of winter and the mouldering foliage of the previous autumn. Some of these delicate flowers actually pierced the dead leaves with needle-like precision. I was so fascinated by this phenomenon that I made detailed drawings of them at every opportunity, beginning with the onion-like bulb below ground and the roots shooting out from it, about which we had learnt at school, and finishing with the little leaf which hovered protectively over the fully developed bell-shaped flower. Snowdrops were followed in quick succession by all the other Spring flowers, pale yellow primroses and hepatica of a delicate blue shading into mauve, giving way to crocuses and to wild violets whose scent could perfume an entire room. Soon the pussy-willows which were blessed at our Palm Sunday liturgy appeared. Since worshippers had to supply their own, before entering for the service each member of the congregation could purchase a small bunch of them from the flower sellers in the church square. Later on, Viennese children would go there for the little bouquet of lilies-of-the-valley with which mothers were greeted on the first of May.

Towards the end of Lent, Fräuli took us to see the "Kalvarienberg" (Mount Calvary) which, as far as I can remember, was an outdoor representation of the Passion story, with miniature figurines that moved mechanically. Writing this now, I also seem to recall the Three Kings travelling towards Bethlehem, and a moving Star which guided them, so perhaps the little dramatic representation tried to span the whole life of Christ. The only details about which I am quite certain are that the view was panoramic, for all events occurred simultaneously, as in a mediaeval work of art. Real drops of blood seemed to fall from Jesus on the Cross. The spectacle was fascinating, but because of its diminutive size, not sufficiently realistic to horrify me.

During the latter part of Holy Week traditional Austrian fare was served at our noon meals. On Maundy Thursday we were always given spinach, presumably because in German the day was known as "Green Thursday" (*Gründonnerstag*). I still have vivid memories of sitting on a little stool after everybody else has finished eating. On a large chair in front of me the creamed vegetable, with a fried egg on top, is congealing into a horrible grey mass, but a certain amount has to be forced down before I am going to be allowed to get up. Lentils, much more appealing because of their piquant flavouring, regularly appeared on Good Friday. During our walk that afternoon, Fräuli would take us into a nearby church where, following a popular mediaeval tradition, at one of the side altars an open sepulchre had been erected, containing a life-sized effigy of the dead Christ. Before this tomb, two boy scouts stood stiffly to attention, clearly representing a guard of honour rather than the Roman soldiers mentioned in the biblical account. The next day we would hear the volley of cannon fire which announced Christ's Resurrection.

Though Spring brought flowers and sunshine, and occasional weekend excursions into the woods, none of these could not compare with summer holidays in my beloved Velden. However all too soon summer faded into autumn, and another school year would summon us back to Vienna to a much more circumscribed way of life which required proper city attire and included unpleasant visits to doctors and dentists. Schoolwork took up much of my time, for not only did we have classes from Monday through Friday until early afternoon, but we also had to attend school Saturday mornings. Once I got back home, Fräuli would take us for a walk, long or short depending on how much of the afternoon was still available. Sometimes this involved accompanying her to shops where she had to take care of various errands. More often we made our way to a park, where long ago the Viennese had dug trenches to repulse the Turkish invaders, and where we sometimes met other children and could roll our hoops along the paths. Rough play was out of the question since one could not step on the grass, and in any case, we were always dressed for being seen in public. On one such occasion, my four-year old brother was somewhat behind Fräuli and myself, when she suddenly observed old gentlemen turning their heads and staring after him in amazement. Investigating as unobtrusively as possible, she discovered that the little fellow was marching along, reciting large portions of Schiller's *Die Glocke* (The Bell), a long poem which opens with the casting of the bell and rehearses the various events in human life when it is rung, including a highly dramatic account of a terrible fire. Since at the time I was much given to declaiming this piece, there was no question as to where my brother had got it!

In late autumn, dusk would already be falling when we returned home from our walk. The residential Eighteenth District in which we lived had not yet discarded its graceful gas lamps, and so, on the way back, I could watch them being lit. One moment, we were alone in the street, then suddenly, although he seemed to have been invisible before, there would appear a shabby little man with a long-handled implement, who would go from lamp to lamp, prying open the glass lantern which enclosed the wick. Presumably he also turned on the gas, and must have had a small ladder on which to stand, though this I cannot clearly recall. What I still see before me is how, as that shabby figure lit each lamp, a soft glow would magically spread around the area where he had been standing. Immediately, he himself melted away again into the shadows, as he moved on to perform the same service for the next light. Given such a spectacle, twilight was indeed the witching hour! Back from our walk, between supper, homework and bedtime, there was usually still time for playing. We were of course occasionally also taken for afternoon visits to children with whose family my own was well acquainted, and there were always a certain number of birthday parties as well, though secretly I dreaded these. However, protected as we were, we had little opportunity for those spontaneous childhood friendships and casual meetings which are normal today. Consequently my brother and I were thrown together a great deal, a fact which led to considerable understanding between us. Though I sometimes acted the role of the bossy elder sister, and we squabbled like all normal siblings, generally we were good friends and cooperated on many occasions, including games. Naturally the dolls belonged to me, while my brother owned several trains, but usually both of us were involved in playing with these toys. The large celluloid dolls with their eloquent glass eyes had to be baptised, confirmed and married, and these ceremonies demanded as many participants as possible. One poor teddy-bear whom we shared, and who was larger than either of us when we first got him, suffered from extreme ill-health and had to undergo numerous appendectomies! My brother's trains were not of the modern electrical variety, and therefore I was needed to lift the barriers at level crossings so that the carriages could pass; occasionally too, some assistance was called for when they got stuck in a tunnel. Only over construction projects did we part company. While my brother worked, first with simple sets made of wood and later with much more elaborate metal ones, I buried my nose in a book.

Winter never lasted very long. At school we learned songs which urged this season to depart as swiftly as possible, and complained about its cold and whistling wind, but except for the inconvenience of gaiters and galoshes, warmly bundled up, one did not need to mind the weather. Now, as we pursued our daily walk, in certain streets we would encounter swaddled figures, huddling around a small glowing stove, in which chestnuts or special elongated potatoes were roasting. While both were considered delicacies, naturally we preferred the former, and occasionally received a screw of paper containing a few chestnuts, deliciously hot and slightly charred, which could not be eaten right away without burning one's fingers. Of course, we always did! Winter also brought ice-skating and tobogganing, a sport I did not like at all because one shared the sled with others who were always more adventurous than I and who positively enjoyed steep, swift descents. The skating rink, however, was different. It was quite near us and therefore, as I grew older, I was allowed to go there by myself. Freed from adult scrutiny, I could develop at my own pace, so that eventually I had gained considerable confidence and actually enjoyed skating as fast as possible in my orange costume.

The best part of this season, however, was Christmas and all that pertained to it. In my mind is still a vague memory of an Advent wreath, containing four white candles, each with its own streamer, three of them violet and one white. I might have seen such a wreath in church; more probably, it was in our classroom Though a harbinger of Christmas, to our childish minds a far more vivid foretaste was the Feast of St. Nicholas, celebrated on 6 December. Even if we did not get a school holiday for it, the occasion remained exciting just the same. St. Nicholas was a stern bishop, robed in full episcopal splendour, with a long white beard, a tall golden mitre, and a great crozier. He was always accompanied by a figure from the nether regions, known as "Krampus". The latter, who was covered with black fur and had a long tail, carried a sack over his shoulder into which he would put naughty children and carry them away – that, at any rate, is what we were told! In the late afternoon of 5 December, coming home from our usual walk, my brother and I could always see the pair of them, walking along some main thoroughfare. Invariably, we tugged hastily at Fräuli's sleeve, begging her to turn quickly into a side-street, but since there seemed to be a multiplicity of bishops and devils abroad at this twilight hour, a different route merely led to yet another encounter. Strangely, this fact did not shake our childish faith; it only frightened us all the more.

After supper, just when we were getting ready for bed, our doorbell rang insistently, and a deep voice could be heard enquiring whether any children lived here, and if they had been good these past twelve months. As soon as the ritual questioning began, we scurried under our beds. What if the answer were "no" ? Then Krampus would carry us off in his sack!! Every year, however, the visitors seemed to receive satisfactory replies and went away again. As soon as we were sure that they had left, my brother and I emerged, carefully set our shoes beside our bed, and in spite of all our excitement, tried to go to sleep as quickly as possible. In the morning, our shoes would be filled with chocolates and sweets. Amidst these, my headstrong brother occasionally also found a lump of coal or a raw potato, reminders that he had been somewhat naughty in the recent past. Always, as a general warning, there was a switch, made of birchrods, but decorated with gaily-wrapped bonbons – their number seemed to depend on how well we had been behaving in the past few weeks! St. Nicholas obviously left the sweets, and Krampus the switch, an instrument which, in fact, was never used and quickly disappeared again. Once these two had visited us, we knew that Christmas was indeed fast approaching, bringing with it the real presents, of which the chocolates were but a foretaste.

If we looked forward to the sixth of December with mixed emotions, Christmas was anticipated with sheer delight. At that time, it was still a feast which was meant especially for children, and which had not yet become commercialised. Each year involved the same ritual. A day or so before Christmas, late in the afternoon Fräuli would take my brother and me to a nearby city lot where we would choose a tall, thick fir-tree which could be loaded on our sled. The mythology of our childhood maintained that it was the Christ child, assisted by his angels, who trimmed our tree; we, however, had to help by bringing it home for him. Once there, the tree disappeared from view and the doors of the dining-room were locked. Furthermore, the key was left on the inside of the lock, circumventing any possible peeking through the keyhole. This was obviously necessary, for the mysterious noises coming from inside over the next twenty-four hours were unbearably tantalising. Heavy objects seemed to be moving back and forth, tissue paper rustled, feet came and went; hushed voices exchanged low murmurs. Since in Austria Christmas is traditionally celebrated on the Eve of the Feast, the 24 December seemed to us the longest day of the year. To keep ourselves amused during the late afternoon, my brother and I frequently settled down to our ancient gramophone which had to be wound by hand and petered out halfway through any record, unless someone cranked it up again midway. Needless to say, we preferred *not* to do so, and revelled in the plaintive whine with which every piece of music came to its untimely halt. Appropriate to the season, we wickedly repeated the song *Alle Jahre wieder, kommt das Christuskind* (Every Year the Christ Child Comes Again) over and over, amused by the way in which the second stanza petered out each time with a wailing "in all his wayeees". No adult ever put a stop to this tomfoolery; obviously they were all busy and glad not to have us underfoot.

Finally, it began to grow really dark outside and we would hear the ringing of the first doorbell which indicated that the Christ child must have come to finish the decorations on our tree and to place all the presents underneath. Later there were repeated rings, announcing the arrival of grandparents, great-uncles and aunts. As the long-awaited moment drew near, we could barely manage to finish our supper. Seated by the window, we would look at the night sky, wondering on which bright star the Christ child would travel home again. Then, suddenly, the double doors were flung wide open and there in the dark room stood a blazing tree, reaching all the way to the ceiling, and topped with a shining silver star. Hundreds of white wax candles threw a steady light, while little sparkling rockets exploded from all sides like miniature fireworks. Sweets that appeared only at Christmas time weighed down the tree, whose scent filled the whole room. Tiny woven baskets, filled with bonbons, hung from the branches, and small meringues, twisted into pretzel shapes, were suspended by a fine golden thread. Among the decorations which shimmered with silver and gold, dainty little angels, dressed in pink or white crêpe paper, swayed gently. They could not be touched because their flaxen hair cut one's skin, but right now we did not want to touch anything anyhow; we only wanted to gaze, overcome by the glorious sight. Invariably eager adults, anxious to see how we liked some special gift, had to remind us about the presents waiting underneath the tree. However, before any package could be opened, and while the tree still held all our attention, the whole family sang the traditional *Silent Night*. Somewhat later my brother and I usually took turns playing a brief piece or two on the piano, to show our fond relations how much progress we had made over the past year. While I plodded conscientiously through whatever was set before me, my brother, who had inherited my mother's musical talent, was already impressing the assembled guests even though his small fingers could barely reach the keys.

Since we did not frequent toyshops or see any advertisements, we had no long wish-list, and most presents were usually a surprise. While I still recall that the aunts and uncles in far away Frankfurt usually sent interesting, thick books, I no longer remember what they were about. Those childhood toys that still live in my mind's eye seem like permanent furnishings of our nursery and are of uncertain provenance. Who gave me my beloved Helene, a doll from my mother's youth, with wonderful long hair and a body that was filled with sawdust which could be spilled all too easily? Was it a gift associated with a visit to my grandparents, or was the occasion my birthday rather than Christmas? And did Fräuli *really* always receive yards of material for a new dress from my parents? There were certainly a great many presents under the tree, all to be treasured and cared for, but the only one that I can clearly associate with Christmas probably appeared in 1937, and certainly not much earlier. During that year my father used his spare time to transform a shoebox into a little general store for me. The hours which he and a medical colleague spent on this labour of love must have given them much satisfaction, for the tiny shop was perfect in every detail. Small scraps of material, wrapped around cardboard, became bales of cloth which I offered for sale on a minute counter; fruit and vegetables could be weighed on a pair of diminutive scales that actually balanced. The shop could be played with for hours and became one of my most favourite toys.

Besides our presents under the tree, there was also a special "Christmas Platter" for each member of the household on the long dining-room sideboard. At no other time could one find such a plethora of good things as were heaped on that Christmas platter! Not only did it hold apples and oranges, nuts, dates and figs, as well as small, fragrant tangerines, but it was also sure to contain a bunch of large and deliciously chewy dried muscatel grapes which the shops only carried at this special season. Moreover, if one was lucky – and we children always were – the oranges on our platter turned out to be "blood oranges", a type whose flesh varied from pink to deep crimson red and had a peculiarly piquant, sweet flavour. Best of all, these delights could be disposed of as we pleased, since the Christmas platter was not subject to the usual rules. In a world where store-bought chocolate bars and chips seemingly did not exist, while pastries were intended for dessert and never stored in tins to be nibbled between meals, such license constituted a rare treat. Yet though the pungent smell of tangerine skins immediately calls Christmas to my mind, it is really our fairy-world tree, present in our house from 24 December until the Feast of the Epiphany on 6 January, that dominates my memories. While each day more of the chocolates and sweetmeats which hung on its boughs disappeared, whenever the tree was relit and bathed in soft candlelight, it retained the illusory magic which I wanted to keep forever. By 1937, however, the faintest hint of changing perspectives was in the air. These presented themselves to my consciousness one afternoon in early December, when my mother beckoned me into her room and said, "Now that you are getting to be a big girl, you can help me". The task which she invited me to share with her involved making paper ornaments for the Christmas tree, and was clearly intended as a privilege, since my brother was excluded from it. Years later, I learnt that as a young girl, she herself had taken great delight in such activities, for even in old age my mother still recalled gilding walnut shells and fashioning them into ingenious little baskets which would be filled with minute sweets and suspended from the branches. At the time, however, I was barely ten years old and distrusted the new, semi-adult role which was being thrust on me, while the suggestion that the Christ child was not solely responsible for the decorations on our tree seemed particularly disturbing. Consequently, as soon as my task was completed, I forgot all about that afternoon; when Christmas arrived a few weeks later – my last real Austrian Christmas, though I did not know it then – its magic still held me entranced as it had always done before.

The faint unease manifested in the above episode was part of a whole realm of questions that troubled me continuously, but could not be discussed with anyone. And therefore this description of the passing seasons, each with its own delights, presents only what was happening on the surface where all childish problems were open to adult scrutiny. However, I was also, as I believe many children are, by nature *anima naturaliter religiosa*, instinctively accepting that there were mysterious forces in another realm, to whom I had to give the right names, and whose rules were to be obeyed. Clearly this was a very sacred realm, which could only be discussed with due reverence, and I feared that other people would not understand this. For no one else, not even Fräuli, seemed to be interested in such matters, which meant that this part of my life had to be hidden from everyone.

As far as I can remember, the first problem I encountered was fairly easy to sort out. Happily, the Latin pantheon corresponded very closely to the Greek one, and once I had established that Jupiter was really Zeus under another name, all the rest fell into place and I was satisfied. However matters became more complicated when I encountered the Norse gods since these could not be neatly arranged in the same way, in spite of my strenuous efforts to match each one with an Olympian counterpart. On the whole, I preferred to stick to Zeus, father of all the gods. Did I relinquish my childhood ambition to become a Greek goddess when such an apotheosis began to seem impossible or was I already less sure about the reality of that mythological heaven? Perhaps both actualities were beginning to seem doubtful. My first encounter with school prayers made me wonder what would happen if one prayed to Zeus instead. It seemed worth trying! However, after a brief attempt to address the latter – in an act of worship rather than with a request of some kind – I grew frightened at my own boldness and hastily withdrew the prayer. I never tried again, for my action seemed dangerously akin to that idolatry which the Christian martyrs had so bravely resisted. Though I continued to love Greek mythology, from now on it would be the dichotomy between what I was being taught in catechism classes and how much of that was or was not being observed at home which would prove so uncomfortable and perplexing.

It could be argued that my official introduction to Catholicism was not exactly the most auspicious one, because before the water of baptism could be poured over my head, I dashed out of the church. Much later I learned how this ceremony had come about, but at the time I understood nothing of what was happening. The fact that I was enrolled in primary school without any denominational affiliation had not really bothered me, though I had wanted to join in the daily prayers and didn't quite understand why I shouldn't do so. However, the matter had been of some concern to my parents, as well as to my maternal grandfather, who thought that since one day I would become a teacher in the Austrian school system, perhaps a professor at a *Gymnasium*, I would fit in more comfortably if I were raised in the state religion. And so, as I dimly recall, a week or so before my brother and I were to be baptised, my mother took me to a church which I had never previously entered, to see a christening. If she offered me any explanation – and she may not have done so – the whole thing went right over my head, for the fact that I was going out with her alone was quite enough to have to cope with.

A week later, my brother and I were both taken to that same church. As the strange, long ceremony progressed, I became increasingly frightened. At the crucial moment, when the water was about to be poured over my head, I bolted. Angrily, my mother wanted to rush after me, but the well known Jesuit who was officiating wisely suggested that he might as well complete the baptism of my younger brother first, meanwhile giving me a chance to calm down. Tradition allowed infants to protest, but what did one do with a kicking, screaming six-year old, soon to be seven?? So for the moment I was left hiding in the walled garden adjoining the church, while two well-meaning nuns did their best to coax me back to the font. They reminded me that I was a big girl now, but of what use was this reminder? It only impressed on me more sharply that my mother would consider that I had publicly disgraced her! Why, oh why wasn't Fräuli there to protect me? If only I would go back, the nuns promised, I would get a little box camera. This argument, however, made even less sense to me, since at my age, I had no interest in cameras. Furthermore I was quite sure that even if someone – even if the nuns – gave me one, my mother would never allow me to keep it. The nuns didn't know my mother. I did! They had no idea how angry she could be! As for the assertion that it wouldn't hurt, grown ups always promised that something wouldn't, and then it did! I wanted more reliable reassurance than that. Fortunately I received it just when I needed it most, for as my mother came out of church to look for me, my newly baptised, four-year old brother ran out into the garden ahead of her and called out, "Don't be afraid Liesl. It's exactly like going to the hairdresser!"

The baptism of my brother and myself was of course only possible because my mother herself had just been received into the Church. Whatever reasons had led her to take this step, in part at least, it was done for the sake of us children. Previously, my mother had not belonged to any religious denomination, though as a school girl she had received some instruction in the Lutheran faith to which her father – our Opapa – belonged, since under the old Emperor, every child had to be raised in some religious faith; however she had never been baptised into the Lutheran faith.

Naturally, these matters were not discussed with us children, and very early I sensed that religion was a taboo subject which grown-ups found embarrassing. I doubt that I even realised that my mother had become a Catholic, any more than I knew that my father had been brought up in the Jewish faith, but had ceased to practise it long before his marriage. Both my parents, but particularly my mother, seemed to be fairly anti-clerical, as was common in a country where religion and politics were so closely intertwined. Much as I longed to go to church regularly, I did not dare ask my mother to take me, and doubt if she herself ever went at that time. Now and then, if the occasion seemed especially important, we accompanied Fräuli, but she too did not seem to think that Sunday Mass mattered very much. In her own peasant fashion, she was mildly sceptical, and told us apocryphal horror stories about convent life, although one such, concerning a superior who would deliberately spill dirt on a floor, just after the novices had carefully polished it, in order to teach them humility and obedience, might have happened at that time. So while a certain amount of traditional Catholic culture, particularly when connected with major festivals, could not help permeating our home, no one there ever encouraged us in any religious observance, and being "good" was always expressed in terms of pleasing one's mother rather than of pleasing God. As far as I can remember, when we were in Velden, we never set foot in a church.

Thus, my religious training, as well as much of its practice, depended entirely on the school room. Even during that first year when I did not belong to any religious denomination, some of the instruction must have rubbed off on me unofficially, for when I was allowed to choose my baptismal name the following September, I requested "Maria" in honour of Mary, the Mother of Baby Jesus. By the second year, most of us were seven years old and were presumed to have reached the age of reason necessary for making one's First Holy Communion. Hence, the weekly instructions by the visiting chaplain were largely devoted to preparations for this great event. Although we worried how brushing our teeth might inadvertently break the Communion fast, and took great pains to shred the piece of paper on which we had jotted our sins for First Confession, finally flushing the bits down the lavatory, I cannot remember ever being frightened by what I was taught, and still possess that charming little book, entitled *Jesus and I*, which introduced us first communicants to the elements of the Mass. On the day of our First Communion, we recited the prayers found on each page aloud in unison, and when the time came for receiving communion, row by row we approached the railing and carefully lifted up the white cloth hanging there and covered up our hands and closed our eyes, because what was about to happen was exceedingly holy. When the ceremony was over, we trooped out as solemnly as we had marched in, looking neither right nor left, though aware that family and friends, as well as casual onlookers, were staring at us. Only one discordant note had been struck, but everyone carefully refrained from referring to it. During our final instructions for First Communion, the young and earnest Chaplain had stressed the need for simplicity of dress, telling us to avoid white frills and lace. No doubt all of us had repeated his words at home. Two mothers, obviously not personally familiar with what this day entailed, had interpreted this warning too literally. Their unfortunate offspring arrived at the central gathering point, wearing ordinary proper party frocks. I remember feeling immensely sorry for these girls, and embarrassed on their behalf, for they were extremely conspicuous amongst the rest of us in our white dresses, veils and gloves. I also remember recognising those party frocks as identical in stuff and pattern with what my mother always chose for me; and that I knew instinctively that the children came from the same background and social class as I did. I was terribly glad that my mother had not made a similar mistake! Whether or not I realised that she too had not really known what this was all about and might easily have put me into the same discomfiting position, I do not know. If I sensed this fact, I suppressed it immediately.

The delightful child-like illustrations in our prayerbook as well as the wording of its prayers clearly show that in all our teaching, love was stressed above fear. Unlike the later Irish-American indoctrination I was to receive, as far as my primary school instruction was concerned, I never needed to unlearn what I learnt in Austria. Much as I secretly longed to go to church regularly, at no time did I suffer feelings of guilt for being unable to do so, though I was always very happy that the school year offered many opportunities for church attendance. Once we had made our First Holy Communion, there were regular sung School Masses for which we learnt simplified Haydn settings, as well as Processions on such feasts as Corpus Christi, when we wore our white First Communion dresses and scattered rose petals before the baldachin, underneath which the priest walked, solemnly displaying the Host in its golden monstrance. I sang happily, though totally out of tune, with my classmates, and took part in all these devotions. In primary school, we covered a fairly substantial amount of Old Testament history, as well as basic catechism. We were also introduced to the early Christian martyrs, about whose sufferings Mamama – my maternal grandmother – could tell me some gruesome stories. My interest in all this must have been obvious, because one day after a school lesson, a boy in my class offered to lend me one of his books from home, suggesting that he would bring it round to me later that afternoon. My discomfort was extreme – I couldn't very well tell him not to come, yet I had never before been allowed to invite an unknown child to visit me, let alone one who came from another social background, something I sensed without having to be told. Nevertheless, his offer was so kind that to this day I remember that he was blond and that his name was Franz. I wonder if his parents too disapproved for somewhat different reasons? In any case, Franz came to our door, carrying the book. I have a vague sense that he had to offer Fräuli all his explanations on the threshold and was not allowed to come inside. The whole episode upset me so much that I barely glanced at his book and returned it as quickly as possible. Here too, there was a subtext that I recognised but did not understand. Why couldn't Franz and I be friends, and why couldn't he visit me? Somehow, both religion and money seemed to be involved in this instance, and neither could be discussed. Though in a slightly different way, the subject of money could be as difficult as the one of religion, as I knew from my problems concerning pocket-money. For though theoretically my father gave me a shilling a week with which I could buy various school items or save up for presents I wanted to give, in practice he forgot to do so most of the time. I felt extremely awkward about asking for money and therefore never reminded my busy father, even though there was no reason to be afraid of him, and he would have been glad to rectify the omission. I felt equally ill at ease about displaying my instinctive natural generosity, and sensed that it might fall under adult censorship. I can still remember an occasion when I deliberately dawdled behind Fräuli so that I could hastily rush up to a beggar and give him a penny. Another time, when I was having my private French lesson at home, and Mademoiselle admired the bouquet of alpine flowers that my mother had picked high in the mountains, I invited her to choose one of them for herself. Needless to say, my mother was thoroughly displeased.

The difference between problems dealing with religion and those concerning money was that the latter only impinged on my consciousness on rare occasions, whereas the practice of religion, and the whole ethos surrounding it, seemed to be woven into the very fabric of my life. Though no one at home encouraged me and I sensed that this whole area of experience was treated with slight mockery, nevertheless my beliefs remained firmly rooted. Of course, I received much support at school, but my favourite books also seemed to confirm some of that teaching. All the Trojan heroes – and the Greeks too, one had to admit – had worshipped their deities, showing that religious observances were commonly practised and considered appropriate behaviour. Furthermore, I had an ally in my younger brother to whom I would pass on whatever I was learning at school, though sometimes this might take a rather odd form. Probably, I was seven and he was four when I introduced him to night prayers, to be said once we were in bed, when no grown-up was likely to interfere any more. However, for some reason I had become convinced that one had to say *all* the prayers that one knew, beginning with the longest (the Creed) and ending with the shortest (the mealtime blessing). If somehow they got out of order, and they seemed to do so rather frequently, then one had to start all over. For some time, night prayers were a considerable burden. In the end, my brother probably protested and we abandoned this system, but we never stopped being firmly united in our own world which ignored the adults around us. We did not foresee that very soon the two of us would quite literally have to stand together alone.

CHAPTER III
GATHERING CLOUDS

My schoolmates and I looked forward to the summer of 1937 and to the completion of our last year in primary school with a mixture of pleasure and fearful anticipation, expecting soon to be faced with stern choices, marking the end of real childhood. Our sense that life was to be taken seriously is reflected in a handsome autograph album, which has somehow survived all my wartime journeys, and is filled with short and flowery maxims carefully written in childish hands. Mostly dating from late 1936, these illustrate that we felt the burden of maturity already on our shoulders and wanted to encourage one another before parting forever. In this we were really only following the example of family members and teachers who contributed the very first entries in the little book, handing out good advice, supported with excerpts from classic German poetry. To be asked to write in someone's album was obviously a sign of favour, but boys were not expected to be interested in such sentimental matters and all the entries I have, most of them decorated with stickers or with drawings of flowers, are made by girls. Each brief verse is inscribed "in happy memory of your classmate", signed in full with a name to which I can often attach, if not a face, then at least certain characteristics. Only one of my schoolmates allowed herself a light-hearted entry; all the rest chose rhymes with extremely serious sentiments, moral, nostalgic or religious.

> True happiness you'll never lack,
> If you look up, forward and back.

says one girl, named Vera G. Vera came from the same social background as I, and had the kind of thick brown plaits for which I longed, especially since my mother made me wear bangs and had my dark brown hair cut very short. Our school books assured us that every true Germanic fairy-tale heroine had long blond braids, and therefore Vera's plaits, though dark and not fair, seemed to me to be much closer to the ideal. That they were not, I only learned later... Another ten-year old, impressed by the gravity of what lay ahead of us, asserts confidently,

> Long after you have bid adieu
> To childhood, and face other spheres,
> May words writ here recall to you:
> "How happy were our youthful years".

As regards sentiment and outlay, this is a typical page from my autograph book. Less typical are several errors, both in spelling and grammar.

Little did we realise that childhood was ending for all of us even more abruptly than anticipated, and for some of us, particularly drastically. There is, for instance, Lily K. who added a bunch of clumsily drawn forget-me-nots to her verses, which tell me that when I'll look at this page with snow-white hair, I'll be able to remember one of the friends of my youth. What fate lay ahead for this daughter of a small Jewish shopkeeper, without money or

influence to obtain the necessary visa? Then there is the classmate
who copies the quotation from the German poet, Friedrich Rückert,
which one of my teachers had already used, and pleads,

> Forgive the friend who hurts;
> Forgive and know 'tis true,
> He is himself in pain
> Else would he not harm you.

Since in our disciplined classrooms not even verbal squabbles
were permitted, and once outside school, we had to go straight
home to what was a totally separate world, I can remember no
occasion which might have given rise to this solemn little
injunction. In retrospect, however, the quotation seems strangely
prophetic, for though we children did not know it at the time, the
Anschluss, the Annexation of Austria, lay just around the corner,
and the deadly virus which Hitler brought with him would infect
most Austrians, who already had a marked propensity to catch
that particular disease. So perhaps the behaviour of my compatriots
could be explained by the fact that they were indeed ill and "in pain";
a knowledge which does not make forgiveness any easier.

As always, once school ended, we spent the summer in Velden,
but leaving again was much harder this time. Weeks before, I
had started scribbling elegiac verses, celebrating the little town.
Now, as the departing train slowly gathered speed, my tears fell
unchecked. "What's the matter with her?", my seven-year old
brother demanded impatiently. "Liesl is sad because we are
leaving Velden", Fräuli told him. He looked puzzled; what was
there to cry about? We came every summer and left every autumn
There was a time for building castles with thick, fine sand, and
there was a time for getting out all the toys which were awaiting
us in Vienna. I knew all that too, and therefore could not give any
reason why I cried so inconsolably that late August in 1937. Today
I know only too well why I shed such bitter tears at the end of
that summer, for seven months later, the Nazis invaded Austria. I
have never again seen the little town, which nowadays is
supposedly a very fashionable spa. Does anyone there still
remember the beggar-gypsies or the Don Cossack Choir? Hitler
eradicated the one, Stalin the other. As far as I can recall, I had never
before cried when leaving Velden, nor does it seem likely that I
would ever have done so again, had future summers brought me
back there. Hence, in the light of what happened, my foreboding
heart seems strangely significant, and these tears, seated on the

upholstered bench of our second-class train compartment, are the most vivid memory that I have of 1937.

If the established pattern had not been broken so irretrievably, perhaps other memories would have predominated. After all, the Vienna-bound train was carrying me to a brand new school that autumn. I can remember neither apprehension nor excitement, and yet usually every new challenge and every change in routine terrified me. In fact, for this very reason, I was now going to a school which in those days, girls of my class and academic abilities did not normally attend. For despite my excellent record during the previous four years, I had been so afraid of the entrance exam to the *Gymnasium*, that for once my mother had allowed me to postpone the dreaded ordeal. In fact the pædiatrician, considering my frequent illnesses in the past, had urged this course, while teachers must have stressed that in any case I was ahead of myself since I had started school before my sixth birthday. Hence the year's respite. The *Gymnasium* I should have attended would have been closer to home, next door to the primary school to which I had become accustomed, but now I had a slightly longer walk to the nearest public high school for girls, designed for those of the poorer classes. Even though my year there was cut unexpectedly short, I ought to be able to remember something of that time. Did I fit into my classroom? I can't recall any sense of strain, yet children of my generation were highly sensitive to all social nuances. Or were others like me there, just putting in a year? No name or face rises out of that particular bit of my past, nor can I recall the girl who made the only new entry into my autograph album. However a certain Marianne C. warns me in tones somewhat less serious than those we had adopted in our last year of primary school,

> Too deep into the inkwell of the world don't dip,
> Or else across the book of life a blot might slip

This entry is dated February 1938, the same month in which the school issued me a formal, semi-annual certificate, replacing the single annual report card which, in primary school, had been filled in twice a year. Such half-yearly certificates must have been normal in a high school which young people, once they had reached the required age, might quit at mid-term to join the work force. Since I too, belong among those who had to leave before the scholastic year was over – and under traumatic conditions which have affected my memory of the time I spent at the school – today I am glad to have some record of my attendance there.

The autumn of that new school year also brought my tenth birthday which occurred at the beginning of November. My high school report notes that I only missed eleven days of classes, so my health was improving, and with it my appetite, always such a bone of contention at home. While my skating still couldn't match my proficiency in swimming, in the winter of 1937 it was reaching a respectable standard, and one of which my mother could be proud. Furthermore, my report card suggests that I must have been quite happy at school. Like my kindly primary school teachers, so now sympathetic highschool instructors rewarded my efforts at Singing, Gymnastics, Handwriting and Drawing with higher grades than my actual performance warranted, and gave me top grades for the new, combined subject of History and Geography as well as for Religion, German, Maths, and French. This last named subject had always played a useful role in our home, for whenever they wished to discuss something which we children were not meant to hear, my parents would switch to French. Now, however, because of my increasing proficiency, they had to turn to English instead. I was fascinated by the sounds of this new language and by the strange pronunciation of its vowels. One day, my mother demonstrated how one said "baby" in English, and then went on to explain that one could actually learn to *think* in a foreign language like English. Though I had been singing French songs since nursery school and was doing reasonably well reading simple little stories, I found this concept very hard to grasp. "In fact", my mother went on to explain, "you can learn to think so well in another language, that you can't think any more in your own. That's what's happened to Adolf. When he writes home to his mother – even though he is writing in German – you can tell that he is really thinking in English." This made no sense to me at all, nor could my mother really explain it any further. However, she went on to tell me more about how this had happened to Cousin Adolf who was a heart specialist, the son of a famous heart specialist, long since dead, who had practised in Frankfurt-am-Main in far away Germany. He had been such a skilled physician, my mother said, that many years ago, the ailing Austrian Empress had sent for him and he had helped her. Though Adolf's father had been content to return home, laden with honours and riches, his son had wanted larger horizons than Frankfurt, a small, provincial city, offered. Consequently Adolf had moved to Vienna, but after some years, feeling that even Vienna was too small for him, he had settled in London where he now enjoyed a very successful practice. This at least was the version my mother presented to me, carefully hiding the fact that the peripatetic career of this cousin – ironically bearing the same first name as Hitler – might have been somewhat influenced by the racial laws which his namesake was promulgating in Germany. Who could guess that Cousin Adolf's foresight would soon stand me in good stead?

Except for feeling a little more grown up and better able to enjoy myself, the winter of 1937 seemed no different from all previous ones. There were always the seasonal feasts to look forward to, and the only faint shadow that briefly disturbed me that Christmas was the intuition that growing out of childhood might involve loss of things I held dear. While Christmas was the children's feast, *"Sylvesterabend"*, New Year's Eve, belonged especially to adults. Naturally we were not included in these parties, but stayed at home with Fräuli and melted battle-weary toy soldiers, endeavouring to decipher the future through whatever new shape the molten lead assumed when we dipped it into a bucket of cold water, though owing to our impatience and lack of skill, the soldiers never quite lost their identity, nor could we produce any meaningful new shape. The following day, everyone, young as well as old, received good luck symbols – little piglets and red toadstools with white spots, both usually made from marzipan. When we went for our customary afternoon walk, we always kept a lookout for a real chimney-sweep, who would have been the luckiest symbol of all. Alas, we seldom met one! Nor would such a meeting on New Year's Day in 1938 have been of much avail.

Once January had begun, Spring was not so far away any more. Soon as usual, all the flowers started appearing in their turn. Suddenly, however, this orderly procession of Nature was disrupted by a different kind of manifestation. One day in early March, tiny, crooked crosses were sprinkled all over the streets along which we took our walk. When I asked how they had got there, Fräuli explained briefly that an aeroplane has dropped them. She seemed to be disturbed by their appearance and would not comment further. The silver crosses sparkled invitingly in the sun, but though I longed to pick up one or two, I was not allowed to touch any of them.

A week later, Fräuli was wearing precisely such a cross in her lapel. She did so most unwillingly, but obviously had to conform. Perhaps she also realised, though we children did not, that her swastika provided a certain measure of protection for my brother and myself, for under her care, we could continue to walk the streets of Vienna unmolested. Adults of whom the Nazis disapproved – all those with a different political ideology and the many considered not pure "Aryan" – were less fortunate, especially male members of these groups who were in constant danger of instant arrest, and while still free often had to cope with public humiliation, the first step in Hitler's extermination plan. Marked for harassment, they were liable to be stopped in the street and forced to scrub the pavement or a public lavatory, often with something like a toothbrush. Thus singled out and ridiculed, in no time at all ordinary citizens could be made to appear "different" and of less worth than their neighbours. Within a day or two of the *Anschluss*, as the Annexation of Austria was called, there was more than enough propaganda to help the process along, and plenty of bully boys to put it into action. Dimly I guessed what lay behind the grim humour of my mother's daily injunction to my father on his way to work – "Come home unscrubbed!" These words sounded ominous but were never explained, and this made them all the more frightening.

The patriotism which school had always instilled in us changed direction overnight, as teachers explained that we lived no longer in Austria, but were part of greater Germany now. We should be proud of being German! So far all our geography and history lessons had concentrated on Austria, and Germany had been described as a foreign country, a distant neighbour about whom to date, we had learnt almost nothing in school. At home and among friends, on the other hand, we had frequently heard Germans mockingly derided, for the Frankfurt dialect was considered rather a joke, while the accent and manners of the stiff Prussians struck the easy-going Viennese as ridiculous. Though the transformation of Austria into Germany was hard to understand, we were accustomed to the adjectival use of "German" in place of "Austrian", especially in patriotic songs. Because the long and cumbersome adjective that denotes being Austrian (*österreichisch*) was too awkward for singing, the monosyllabic adjective for German (*deutsch*) was used instead, and applied to any Germanic people, as well as to the German nation as such. After the disintegration of the old Austro-Hungarian Empire, all that remained of our small country was clearly such a Germanic entity. Consequently the first stanza of our national anthem could implore heaven to bless Austria, and at the same time describe the love and labour of its people as possessing the best "German" qualities. Similarly, the anthem in which we used to praise our "martyred" Chancellor Dollfuss, stated that he had shed his blood for Austria because he was a true "German" hero! Thus we were accustomed to managing without the specific adjective which connoted our national identity. Now, however, we were losing the noun as well, and with it, the words of our own national anthem in our school prayerbooks.

When we outgrew our First Communion prayerbooks, we had been given different ones, which included more grown-up prayers as well as catechetical instruction, and could be used for the rest of our school days. These fat little black books also contained hymns for various occasions and simplified Mass settings; on the very last page was the Austrian national anthem with its familiar Haydn tune, first composed for the Austrian Emperor. Now, within a very short time, we were issued new prayerbooks, identical with the old ones, but omitting the national anthem. I cannot remember how the switch came about, but still possess one of the new books, though oddly enough, the offending last page, obviously torn out from the old prayerbook, is tucked into it. How did I get hold of this page? Was I instinctively preserving something of the past or was I secretly resisting the new regime? For all of us children, the sudden changes must have been confusing. Yet even if we had wanted to ask questions – which we were not accustomed to doing – there was never any opportunity for them. Our teachers were much too busy telling us about the greatness of Germany and describing the wonderful changes that our country was about to experience. The first and most obvious one in the classroom was that we had to learn a number of new patriotic songs. Only a short while before, we had been told that Dollfuss had saved us, though what from we had never found out; now our teachers explained that Hitler had come to save us. The name of Dollfuss disappeared as if it had never existed, and instead we were expected to sing about someone called Horst Wessel, also a "martyr", who was leading us to a brighter future. The song about him, like all the others we learned, had a very appealing tune which could not help stirring one's blood, making one wish that one could instantly join all those comrades in a brisk march. Whenever I went home from high school, past the *Gymnasium*, I could see that the bigger girls were doing exactly that. Never before had they spent so much time on gymnastic drills.

In my own school too, the girls seemed to be occupied with different activities now which somehow, I no longer fully shared.

Instead, during school hours, I was allowed to draw or to paint whatever I liked and no one appeared to supervise my efforts. When I brought one of these works of art home, however, my mother was horrified. "Look at this," she said to my father, "a sunset! Dear God, what will they think?!" Her voice contained the same grim irony that I had heard her use before. Vaguely I wondered why the Germans would object to sunsets, but since my reading had already acquainted me with literary symbols, I half guessed the implication. Therefore, though I enjoyed painting flaming suns setting between dramatic mountain peaks, and had no idea how to suggest their rising instead, when my mother warned me that from now on I had better depict the sun as rising rather than as setting, reluctantly I promised to do so, sensing what was at stake.

As far as my future school activities were concerned, my mother need not have worried, for the very next day, I ceased to be allowed to attend the school. Some time in the morning, the Principal sent for me. Never before had I been in his office, and my knees felt weak with fright, especially since I sensed that his questions were important. Was either one of my parents Jewish, he asked. I didn't know. I didn't think so. What about my grandparents? Again, I didn't know. In fact, I didn't really understand what I was being asked. I was told to go home for the right answers. I can still remember running all the way from school and then back again, but I have no idea what my mother said to me and presumably repeated her words in parrot-like fashion. I know that I spilled them out breathlessly, my voice shaking with fear and haste, and a strange buzzing in my ears. For the first time in my life, I seemed to be two people, for my one self could hear with what a queer, tight voice my other self was speaking, without being able to do anything about it. The information I brought back meant nothing to me. However it meant a great deal to the Principal, who sent me home again, this time for good. He spoke firmly but quite kindly; I think that he even added how sorry he was that I could no longer stay in the school. Bewildered and unable to say goodbye to any of my class mates, I left, still trembling, with the world that I had hitherto known suddenly swept away. What was happening and why? Considering the increasingly hazardous situation, my mother tried to offer me some explanations, but I found it difficult to grasp them, for like most children, I thought in terms of absolutes, and thus was puzzled how I could be both a Catholic *and* a Jew! Furthermore, like many other families in Austria and Germany, ours seemed to be totally assimilated into the Gentile world, and consequently I had never associated the word "Jewish" with any member of it. According to our catechism instruction, if ever I had to suffer persecution for my faith, then I would have to die heroically, as the early Christian martyrs had done. That would be a glorious privilege, freely chosen by me. To be persecuted now for something over which I had no sort of control seemed grossly unfair!

Thus, both school and home had taught me to assume that being Jewish meant belonging to a different religion. There had been one or two such children in my primary school who did not have to come to classes on Saturday morning because, so our form mistress told us, they attended their special religious instruction instead. They seemed to be very poor and I hardly knew them, though Lily's little bunch of forget-me-nots in my autograph-book suggests that we must have exchanged a few words occasionally. Vera G., the girl with the dark braids, and a number of other children like myself, all had recognisably "Jewish" surnames, though we ourselves did not realise this at the time. We were the offspring of families which had lost their Jewish roots at least two generations earlier, without developing any deep Christian ones. Since Hitler's ruthless extermination policy had not yet been fully developed, I might have been able to complete my school year if my mother had brought me to the font at birth, thus making me a "cradle" Catholic. I would have had even more security, if at least on one side of the family, my parents and grandparents had been baptised into some Christian denomination instead of merely receiving perfunctory instruction in their youth, or undergoing a nominal conversion process later in life. Now, although I was, what Caryll Houslander in her autobiography describes as a "rocking-horse" Catholic, this did not seem to count at all. Whatever the deficiencies of my nursery, as a normally intelligent, naturally devout child, at school I had quickly absorbed all the religious instruction with which children my age were familiar. Furthermore, I had made my First Communion at the right age in the second grade, along with all the other children – *and* in a proper white dress! – and so I could not understand in what way I was not simply a Catholic like my other schoolmates.

Today I live in that cultural mosaic called Canada, where people are far more concerned with the individual than with his family background. Obviously, a child of established, well-known parentage can expect to be initially assessed in terms of the home from which it comes. But since the neighbours are primarily interested in the New World and its history, an unknown great-grandfather will matter little to them, unless he happened to be a pioneer in this land. Furthermore, the increased mobility and sheer size of North America enable all newcomers to cut themselves off from their origins and to establish an entirely different adult identity here, if they wish to do so. Two well-known Canadians invented fictitious biographies for themselves, and were completely accepted in the guise in which they chose to appear: Grey Owl, an Englishman living out boyhood dreams, turned himself into a Canadian Indian; passing as such, he did much both for the native peoples and for wildlife conservation, while his delightful books are still popular on both sides of the Atlantic, especially among the young. Frederick Philip Grove, a German immigrant with a somewhat dubious past, claimed to be a Scandinavian with vaguely aristocratic connections. As well as having a certain impact on the educational policies of his day, in Canada he was able to fulfill his literary ambitions and wrote numerous novels about early life on the Prairies. Neither author's *persona* was unmasked in his lifetime, because in this New World the present matters more than the past, and one is judged on current performance. Today we know the real names and identities of these two authors only because their work was of sufficient literary significance to attract scholarly scrutiny. Thus, in this part of the New World, no one is considered a Jew who does not have some genuine affiliation with a Jewish community, or bears an obviously Jewish name. One need not be actively involved in religious practices or observe all the holy days, and one may never buy Israeli Bonds or belong to any Jewish organisation, but at least one will have friends whose children make their Bar Mitzvah, and one will attend such celebrations; at worst, one will angrily and loudly disown one's Jewish heritage while writing exposés decrying the treatment of Palestinian Arabs. None of this could be said to apply to me since my father changed his name when he acquired a new citizenship, and such struggles as I have had with my personal background have centred around problems related to my Christian denominational affiliation. Therefore most North American friends, particularly those who have been settled here for several generations and are not influenced by European thinking, question any attempt to describe myself as Jewish, now that I am finally able to discuss this taboo subject with them. While all the imprinting of my European childhood insists that they are wrong, their refutation makes sense since word and deed should go hand in hand. Nevertheless, anyone of my age and background will always be left wondering how one could both be and *not* be a Jew.

In the Hitler-dominated Austria of 1938 there was no question, of course, about where I belonged. According to the racial laws promulgated by the Nazis, both sides of my family were suddenly considered Jewish. This was more understandable as far as my paternal background was concerned since the religious affiliation of the grandfather whom I had never known and the grandmother whom I could barely remember had, in fact, officially been Judaism, though I doubt that they were particularly observant Jews. One could hardly be a physician in the Austro-Hungarian Army and observe dietary laws! Even if my father had received the customary boyhood instruction of Judaism, he had long since ceased to practise its tenets. However, on legal documents pre-dating the Nazi period, which would have accepted the affirmation that he belonged to "no religious denomination", he is described as being Jewish, nor had he changed his surname which was an obviously Jewish one. My mother's family – at least the branch to which she belonged – had deliberately discarded any Jewish associations, and felt uncomfortable about any second and third cousins who maintained them. Opapa and Mamama, who were related, had a surname which was not obviously Jewish, and particularly disliked orthodox Judaism, as well as any ostentatious display of wealth that might be labelled "Jewish", considering the taint of such blood a dark and shameful secret in the family closet. Opapa was officially Lutheran, while Mamama, despite her gruesome stories about the early Christian martyrs, belonged to no religious denomination. Their three daughters, of whom my mother was the youngest, had been raised in the same way as I had been, with no awareness of the family skeleton, only to discover in late adolescence how and why their social circle seemed to be circumscribed in a Vienna which had always been tarnished by anti-Semitism. I, of course, had an even more rude awakening, as well as a genuine religious upbringing which made for greater complexities.

Before the First World War, Opapa had sat on the Board of Trade, and had been an important and respected member of the Viennese mercantile establishment. Occasionally he had been asked to address their assemblies, and had been known to tease the learned gentlemen by quoting spurious references from Goethe. In those days, the family had been extremely wealthy, with French mademoiselles and English misses for the instruction of the daughters, and a host of family servants. In the opposite apartments lived the owner of the house, a Herr Baron Gutman von Gelse whose coachman and carriage would frequently wait for him in the courtyard, unaware that a small girl, my mother, was gazing down at the fine horses with wistful admiration. Like all members of the nobility, the Herr Baron engaged in hunting, while my grandfather occasionally received game from clients and friends. My mother still recounts with amusement the rivalry between the two cooks, as they gazed out of their respective kitchens across the courtyard and compared the venison each had hung out. 1918 changed all that. Various foreign firms, mainly Czech ones, felt free to disregard their debts to Vienna, and Opapa almost ruined himself, personally seeing to it that all the creditors were paid off. Now he was semi-retired, though the firm must still have been in existence, for I can remember that occasionally I was given sizeable scraps of material – probably trade samples – and that these strange and exotic laces, shot through with gold or silver thread, bedecked my dolls whenever they were confirmed or married. With the end of the war, certain social barriers loosened, for I suspect that otherwise my mother would not have been allowed to marry my father, someone from an insignificant family and with an obviously Jewish name. Still, Opapa had enough influence left so that my father, who really would have preferred human contact to administrative duties, was given the directorship of the private hospital which took so much of his time. Opapa also exercised a decisive voice in my own future, not only by developing my own early love of learning, but also in regard to the religious up-bringing he advocated for me. He himself was steeped in the humanities, and would have been happier pursuing private study to taking his place in the family firm, had any other brother been able to carry the burden instead.

Now, overnight, my mother's distinguished family was branded with the stigma of being Jewish, and hence I was considered a "full-blooded" rather than a "half" Jew, and expelled from school. Had they wanted to do so, my parents could have let me attend a high school which had been set aside for Jewish children, but all other state schools were closed to me. This segregated school, an old building in a poor district, was a long way from home and naturally my parents did not want to send me there. Hence, a few days later, I was enrolled in a private convent school within easy walking distance and along familiar streets. My mother, as well as Fräuli, warned me that if I were stopped on my way to or from school, I should not tell anyone where I was going. Whether a parent complained, or whether someone who questioned me reported the situation – for I can dimly remember inquisitive neighbours down the street, and I was incapable of lying – in less than a week I had to stop attending classes, but at least was allowed to receive private instruction from one of the younger nuns who treated me with great kindness. Amidst vague impressions of my time at the convent school, my most vivid memory concerns the performance of a play which the girls put on towards the end of term which, though I could not join in, I was invited to see. The piece must have been some version of *Coppelia*, for it appeared to take place in a toyshop, where large dolls came to life whenever their creator wound them up. The girls looked very strange in their stage make-up, and their gestures and dance were deliberately mimed, rather than realistic. While I was fascinated by this spectacle, since I had never before been to a theatre, and the state schools I had so far attended did not have any tradition of school plays, what struck me as even more strange was the off-stage behaviour of the performers. From where I was sitting, I could clearly see girls in the wings, waiting their turn to go on and whiling away the time by talking with one another, gesticulating from one side of the stage to the other, using sign language. Watching these clandestine conversations not only shattered the stage illusion for me, but also left me wondering how the girls could care so little about what they were doing. Since they didn't appear to be afraid of being seen and punished, obviously their school world was very different from the one I had known!

My one clear memory of those convent lessons is that for geography I had to study the map of Europe, learning where all the countries were situated, and memorising their capital cities. Perhaps through the only means available to her, my well-intentioned instructor was trying to widen my outloook and to prepare me for life beyond my present national boundaries.... Since my attendance there was totally unofficial, the convent school, of course, could not issue any valid report card for me. Therefore, to qualify for promotion into the next grade, at the end of June I had to present myself for examination at the girls' high school, set aside for Jewish children. The classroom was dark and crowded, and the different teachers, who examined me in the various subjects, were all strange to me. Oddly enough, I cannot remember feeling particularly frightened; perhaps by this time even a child had other, more important things to worry about! I still have the official Examination Report issued by the school, on which, as usual, I was given the top "Very Good" for all academic subjects, and a charitable "Good" for Gym and Singing. Geography was the one exception this time, for whatever curriculum the high school had followed, European countries and their capitals had not been on the syllabus; I think that it was rivers and mountains – probably those of Germany. Consequently, though I coped easily with everything else, I could not answer any of these questions. Under normal circumstances, I would have failed Geography with an "Inadequate", but the sympathetic examiner let me pass with an "Adequate", my lowest mark in five years. I hardly noticed what previously would have been considered a disgraceful blot on my record, while my poor parents, despite all the uncertainty surrounding my future schooling, only wanted to make sure that I received the necessary certificate for advancing to the next grade.

Amidst all the external turmoil around me and the tension at home, hardest of all to cope with was, of course, my internal confusion. Suddenly I no longer knew who I was or where I belonged. The imaginary world which I inhabited most of the time was that of the epic heroes and contained only two classes of people: warriors and slaves, the conquerors and the bondsmen. Foremost among all virtues ranked pride and courage – *nothing* had swayed Hector from going forth to meet the blood-thirsty Achilles! Since my greatest desire was still to right the wrongs of Troy, captured through deceit and treachery, obviously I belonged among the heroes and warriors, yet now suddenly, I found myself denounced as a Jew, and then bombarded with propaganda, suggesting that Jews were mean, cowardly and despicable. On my way to school, on our afternoon walks with Fräuli, everywhere in Vienna there had always been street-corners with kiosks, displaying advertisements and public notices; at almost every tram-stop there were hoardings and placards. Since the *Anschluss*, all these promulgated the crudest form of anti-Semitism in cartoon and story form, and naturally I read it all, as I read every other piece of printed material that came my way, whether or not I understood a word of it. The sensationalism could not help but appeal to me, even though one part of my mind realised that I should not be reading such stuff. Jews were treacherous, these stories said, and reported examples of "pure" Aryans, whom they had tortured and murdered merely out of spite. The Aryans were noble; in fact they possessed all the qualities of my Trojan heroes, whereas the Jews, who had a slave mentality, were an alien, undesirable people who did not belong into the new, glorious Germany, which the most honest among them would themselves admit. Jewish women were just as bad, as you could tell if you observed them in any public vehicle, where you would always find them with their knees spread apart in a most disgusting way, drawing attention to themselves. (The implications of this charge escaped me of course – but wasn't Fräuli always telling me to keep my legs neatly together??)

How much of all this did I believe? Obviously enough to confuse me, for the picture of Germans as warriors and heroes seemed to match reality: it fitted their conquest of Austria, their marching armies, and their stress on health, strength and gymnastics. I did not want to be one of them, but I longed to share all those characteristics. And Jews? Well, quite aside from the fact that I did not want to be cowardly and treacherous, I still did not really understand how I came to be accounted as one of them, when I was really a Catholic. Furthermore, all the propaganda about Jews did not seem to relate in any kind of way to members of my own family, though the warning which my mother issued to my father about coming home "unscrubbed" frightened me, for it suggested being despised and humiliated. Whatever else, I wanted to remain proud, so when Fräuli took us into the park, I held my head high and looked other children straight in the eye, daring them to despise me.

Undoubtedly my parents were aware of some of these problems and therefore, now that the school year was over, they were anxious that my brother and I leave Vienna which was currently engaged in a far more vicious orgy of anti-Semitism than any other region under Nazi control. Though frantic arrangements were already under way to get us children out of the country, these could not be completed quickly enough, and meanwhile, paradoxically, we would be far safer in Germany which, compared to the recently annexed Austria, seemed relatively peaceful. Despite some restrictions, my mother's eldest sister and several other close members of the family lived quite comfortably in Frankfurt-am-Main, and were willing to take us for an indefinite stay. Thus it came about that in the summer of 1938 we embarked on a very different journey from those of previous summers; accompanied by a grown-up cousin, a handsome, strapping girl who was Viennese by birth but had lived with our Frankfurt relatives for some time, my brother and I set out on a long train journey across a frontier that no longer existed.

CHAPTER IV
TEMPORARY REFUGE

Although my brother and I spent almost four full months in Frankfurt, my memories of living there are clouded and fragmentary, enhanced by all too few photos. Apparently this quiet provincial town – as Frankfurt seemed to be in those days – had not yet changed drastically under the Nazi regime, or if it had, this fact did not obtrude into our lives as obviously as it had done in Vienna. Consequently our stay was happy, secure among indulgent aunts and uncles, with only an occasional reminder that even here our situation was precarious. Sometimes my own self-consciousness produced such a warning signal – thus I remember accompanying my aunt soon after our arrival and automatically saying "*Grüss Gott*" when entering a shop, though scarcely had the words left my mouth, when I started wondering what everyone there would think of me. "Grüss Gott" was the traditional, common greeting in Austria, and having used it now in Frankfurt immediately brought to my mind a piece of Nazi propaganda I had seen in Vienna about benevolent German families providing holidays for needy Austrian youngsters. These children, so the news report claimed, could always be recognised by their "*Grüss Gott*" to which their German hosts would respond with kindly smiles. Would the shopkeeper mistake me for that kind of child or consider me an imposter? On another occasion, I started half-singing, half-declaiming Schumann's famous ballad about the two French grenadiers who finally return from Russian captivity, only to learn that Napoleon, their beloved Emperor, has been defeated and exiled. Their heroic sentiments, the pathos of their situation, and the stirring finale in which a triumphant *Marseillaise* is heard above the original tune, strongly appealed to my imagination. Hastily, my aunt and uncle interrupted this outdoor performance, which was all too audible to inquisitive neighbours, and although at that moment I did not remember how my mother had stopped me from painting sunsets, my reactions to the present injunction were much the same. I did, and did not, quite understand, and felt profoundly uneasy as well as somewhat frustrated since this was one of my favourite songs, and though slightly off-key, I had been giving a lusty rendition of it.

Such incidents, however, were isolated. In general, what I really remember best about Frankfurt is its pleasant, countryfied atmosphere for unlike Vienna, where everyone lived in large urban flats, surrounded by anonymous concrete, here people had houses and gardens. Instead of carefully supervised afternoon walks or going to the public park, one simply stepped outdoors to play! Even the somewhat cramped quarters which I shared with Onkel Max and Tante Trudi in the Marienstrasse were part of an ordinary house, quite different from our flat in Vienna which could only be reached via an endless, spiral stone staircase. Whereas here no one was always telling me to hurry up, at home, as soon as dusk began to fall, one could never dawdle because on every landing one had to press another button, so that the next flight of stairs would be briefly illuminated. Tante Trudi was my mother's eldest sister, and though she had never had any children of her own, she and Onkel Max were very fond of me, their only niece. However they were not prepared to have me underfoot all the time, nor wanted me to bury my nose in a book the whole day, and therefore frequently sent me to play with my brother who lived close by in the spacious old family house in the Leerbachstrasse which belonged to Onkel Martin and Tante Grete. The latter had already raised their orphaned nephew – whose elder sister had just accompanied us on our journey from Vienna to Frankfurt – and consequently were much more used to energetic little boys; in fact, they knew far better how to cope with children than did kind Tante Trudi who was a little pedantic and fussy, rather like an elderly spinster schoolmistress. In fairness to her I should add that she was also under considerable pressure, catering to her husband's somewhat irascible temperament which had not been improved by the fact that since 1933, though he was an eminent psychiatrist, he could no longer remain in charge of the great German clinic which he had headed for so long. Poor Onkel Max must have felt very frustrated, cut off from his work, and often left his study to visit Onkel Martin. The two were brothers, very different in character, but with a close bond between them; they were related to us by blood as well as by marriage. The more even-tempered Onkel Martin was a corporation lawyer, and a man of scrupulous rectitude, with a deep love of German classical music and literature, who placed all his faith in German law and German justice, convinced that these would ultimately prevail over Hitler's racial statutes. Thus far, neither brother had thought of emigrating, and the family house seemed solid and secure.

Besides suggesting stability, the Leerbachstrasse house was constructed in an interesting way, for the upper storey included a

large roof-garden which was built out at the back, over the
downstairs quarters. The occupants of the lower part of the house
had their own fenced-in garden as well. I can no longer remember
who lived downstairs, but clearly recall that Martin and Gretl
(as the latter was familiarly called by the grown-ups) were
upstairs, since one had to go through their living-room to reach
the roof-garden. I was fascinated by this phenomenon, for never
before had I seen a garden *on top* of a house, a garden from
which one could look down into another garden below! For us
children, this area became a large playroom. It contained a small
wooden structure, white-washed and latticed, which was part
pavilion, part tool shed; and since my brother showed an early
aptitude for construction and mechanics, Onkel Max and Cousin
Albert, the almost grown-up nephew who had been living with
Onkel Martin and Tante Grete since his mother's death, spent
much of their time up there with him. I, on the other hand, was
more often to be found in the study with Onkel Martin who
continued to foster my interest in German literature, already
inculcated in me by my grandfather, though now I was progressing
from dramatic declamations of Schiller to the more demanding
poetry of Goethe. Tante Trudi also took my education in hand,
for I distinctly remember reading a French translation of *Uncle
Tom's Cabin* with her, but besides having to struggle with the
language at that advanced level, I also found the whole story
incredibly boring. Obviously Harriet Beecher Stowe's respect
for human life and personal dignity was highly relevant in a Nazi
Germany which denied these values, though understandably, that
point went completely over my head.

   In addition to these two sets of uncles and aunts, we were
soon introduced to Cousin Adolf's mother, Tante Louise. The latter
was a regal old lady who lived in a very grand house, set in a
tree-filled garden which to us children seemed more like a park.
While Onkle Max and Tante Trudi's household only contained
one unobtrusive, faithful maid, and Onkel Martin and Tante Grete
had a fat, jolly red-headed cook named Erika, Tante Louise
employed numerous servants, including a chauffeur and a mild-
mannered lady companion whom we called "Tante Dora". My
brother and I were frequently invited to visit Tante Louise, who
displayed an unfailing interest in whatever we were doing and
treated us with great courtesy and kindness. Whenever Tante Dora
suggested that Tante Louise needed to rest now, or had to busy
herself with something else, there were always numerous other

ways in which we could amuse ourselves, exploring the big house, bothering some long-suffering servant, or disappearing into the expanse of garden. The latter was our special delight, for throughout that summer in Frankfurt, as in all the holidays of my Austrian childhood, the sun never seemed to stop shining and the air was always shimmering with heat. The big old trees, under whose shade one could quickly cool off, became our benign guardians. Of particular interest to us were the beeches with their rich harvest of triangular kernels which could be extracted and eaten; provided that one did not gobble each single one up right away, but exercised restraint and saved up several for a proper mouthful, one was rewarded with a sweet, chewy taste. Less wise than the squirrels, occasionally we belaboured some nut left over from the year before, only to find a hard shrivelled kernel inside, scarcely bigger than the head of a pin. Happily, such disappointments were only momentary, since the new crop was exceedingly plentiful, putting a large private hoard entirely at our disposal.

The fact that my mind jumps from the cooling shade of the beech trees to their edible nuts suggests that summer merged into autumn without any awareness on my part, but how could it have been otherwise for us children, since the normal rhythm of our lives had been shattered? As in Vienna, so here in Frankfurt, ordinary schools were closed to us, though in these new surroundings we were much less conscious of this fact. At some point in our stay – probably from early September on – my brother and I, together with a few other children, started attending private handicraft lessons in a large basement workshop, where we were introduced to basic carpentry. I still remember being shown how to handle proper big saws and making a fat, star-shaped candlestick as a home-coming present for my parents, for it seemed very likely that we would be returning to Vienna in late autumn. Though neither instructor nor fellow pupils have left any imprint on my mind, the pleasure of working with wood, which I encountered there for the first time, has remained with me to this day. The aunts and uncles also tried to find other ways to supplement our interrupted schooling, mainly through an increasing amount of structured reading, as well as through various cultural expeditions, which I can dimly remember. We certainly visited the famous *Römer*, a public building whose foundations probably dated back to Roman times, though I can recall nothing of its historical significance and have retained merely a vague impression of palatial high ceilings. My only vivid memory centres around the felt slippers which each one of us had to put over our shoes before being allowed to walk on the old, highly polished oak floors, and which we chose from the various sizes placed at the entrance. The *Goethehaus*, on the other hand, has left even less of an imprint on my mind; for the poet lived for me only in his work, and therefore I could not envisage his existence apart from his poems, no matter how elegant his private house might have been.

Part of the fascination associated with all these excursions was caused by the fact that to reach our destination, we had to go past the Bockenheimergasse, a small street which contained numerous food shops, and therefore was popularly known as the "Fressgasse", best translated into English as "Street for Stuffing Oneself", a sobriquet which always struck us children as hilariously funny. Is that why I still remember the nickname, or is it because increasing difficulties over obtaining provisions were impinging on my developing appetite? I know that I enjoyed all the meals served in Tante Trudi's home, even though they were different from what I was used to, and have especially fond memories of freshly baked carp in sour cream sauce, a festive dish to which I was first introduced in Frankfurt, where fish was much more plentiful than in land-locked Austria. Balancing that recollection, however, is Hitler's institution of the "Eintopftag", the day on which, instead of the usual filling soup, followed by meat, potatoes and vegetables, and of course dessert, the patriotic cook was expected to serve only a single dish, presumably some sort of meatless stew. Furthermore, for every five chicken eggs that she was able to obtain, the German housewife also had to buy one large duck egg, whose faint greenish-white hue was not very appetising. I asked Erika once what this egg tasted like, and she did not seem to think too much of it, though I am not sure whether she used it up in cooking, or simply discarded it. The knowledge that one was forced to buy such a horrid egg, and that it was there in the kitchen – whether or not it ever appeared on our table – was thoroughly unpleasant. Occasionally, distant relations or friends of my aunt and uncle included me in an invitation for tea or for supper, and towards the end of our stay in Frankfurt, Tante Trudi, fearful that without extra sustenance I would eat too much wherever we were going, always gave me bread and jam before leaving home. Although my aunt must have invented some kind of explanation for this strange treat – without admitting that her real concern was due to spinsterish prudery, or perhaps caused by consideration for friends faced with increasing difficulty over food supplies – not only can I no longer remember what she said, but at the time I would have been considerably puzzled by her words. For years, the mere thought of having to go anywhere for a visit had made me sick with anxiety; watchful grown-ups had always surrounded me, to check on the minute spoonfuls I was choking down, painfully afraid that they wouldn't stay put, as indeed most of the time they didn't. Now that at long last I was able to meet adult expectations, I was proud of my healthy appetite and expected praise rather than anxious scrutiny.

Though my timing seemed inconvenient, this growing interest in food was very understandable, since I was approaching my eleventh birthday. The day itself, however, early in November, was scarcely recognised because all celebrations awaited my mother's arrival, which was imminently expected, presumably to take my brother and me back to Vienna. Some time earlier, while visiting Tante Louise, I had been asked to try on a lovely wool frock, deep blue in colour and of a soft texture, with long, full sleeves and tight cuffs. Tante Dora said that the dress was being made for a little girl she knew, who was about my age and size. Once she was certain that it fitted properly, she could finish it – for the frock was going to have smocking in front, as well as embroidery on the "Russian" collar and on the cuffs. I felt a pang of envy towards the unknown child, never guessing that actually the dress was intended for me, either as a birthday gift or as a going-away present. For once, my uncertainty as regards the specific occasion is not due to the passing of time but to the unforseen circumstances which were about to make us leave Frankfurt in considerable haste and bewilderment; hence, for me, the two events are permanently conflated.

My beautifully embroidered frock, with its slightly exotic Cossack collar, is an apt symbol of what Tante Louise represented to me. Her house is forever associated in my mind with all that is strange and wonderful, though tantalisingly few factual memories remain to support this general impression. Is it true that one had to travel along broad tree-lined boulevards to reach her property? Were my brother and I ever allowed to stay overnight? Perhaps the drives in her long, shiny limousine merely exist in my imagination, reflections of what my mother had told me about earlier days. One event, however, a memorable dinner around the time of my birthday, though probably not directly connected with it, definitely took place. During this impressive feast, course succeeded course in true Victorian fashion – soup, fish, fowl and roast – with sherbet in between to refresh the palate. A substantial sweet followed, and last of all came fruit and nuts. Considering the growing food shortage, only Tante Louise with her strong will and formidable determination could have attempted such a display! The fact that for once her second-best china, a magnificent service with elaborate gold and green dragons, was actually being used, rendered the occasion even more memorable. I have no idea who was seated around the large dining-room table, but I recall an endless array of heavy dishes, huge tureens and serving platters, all decorated with these strange beasts, captured here with no hope of release, forced to chase their own tail forever. The only other formal meals which I had previously experienced – those at my grandparents in Vienna – paled in comparison, while the splendour of Tante Louise's dinner service made ample amends for the fact that she did not have a marble *putti* which I could stroke surreptitiously.

While everyone else was enjoying a post-prandial rest, my brother and I were left to play and soon started to quarrel. Finally one of us began to chase the other; in all likelihood my brother was the one pursuing me, for by now the years between us no longer gave me the advantage, and when angry, he could be very violent. Therefore I was probably seeking help, although I would never have admitted as much, when we eventually burst into the kitchen, one dodging the other, dashing between chairs and running around a big table, stacked high with china. Before either the cook or Tante Dora could put a stop to our chase, we had bumped into the table and knocked over several dishes, leaving two or three shattered on the floor; a cup lost its handle. The sight of this disaster sobered me immediately – this was Tante Louise's second-best china and we seemed to have smashed half of it! No matter how much one of us now blamed the other for starting the quarrel, both of us were really responsible for the broken dishes. Would Tante Louise have to find out before we went back to Vienna? How could we tell her? Was she likely to want her second-best china again very soon and could any of it be mended? Crossly, the cook refused to reassure us, and we withdrew very subdued.

But within a very few days of this misfortune, a far greater catastrophe occurred, which put the question of broken china out of everyone's mind. Three days after my birthday, on 11 November, the infamous *"Krystallnacht"* took place. Overnight, Jewish synagogues were burnt to the ground and business premises were smashed and looted; Jewish males were rounded up and the first deportation to Hitler's Concentration Camps was inaugurated. Suddenly, neither Onkel Max nor Onkel Martin were around, and even Albert had disappeared, though thanks to timely warnings, he was safely hidden away. Instead of the male members of the family, my mother was suddenly there, looking extremely worried, and holding endless private consultations with my aunts. When I wanted to know what was the matter, my mother promised that some day, when I was a little older, she would tell me what had happened; meanwhile, she was taking my brother and me back to Vienna. As yet, nothing was settled about our departure for England, but negotiations with the English Quakers were under way and she hoped that we would be leaving quite soon. We said goodbye to Tante Louise without mentioning the broken china...

Our return to Vienna remains a total blur in my mind. Apparently my parents still lived in our old flat and had not yet been forced to move in with my grandparents, since I have no recollection of encountering strange, unfamiliar streets. As far as I know, our beloved Fräuli was also still there, or at least managed to live nearby so as to be able to see us when we got back. The last entry in my autograph book is a sad little verse in her handwriting:

God's wisdom has decreed it thus,
That all of us must part, alas,
From what we hold most dear.

It is signed by her and dated 15 July 1938, presumably the date when my brother and I were taken to Frankfurt, so clearly she had never expected to see us children again. Now, during this tense period of waiting and making preparations, she was there as much as possible, giving my mother much-needed moral support. The handsome diary which I took to England with me to chronicle my years there contains a brief inscription, stating that it is her parting gift to me. Before this story leaves all my life in Austria behind, I must add that several years later, long after my parents had escaped to the United States, our faithful Fräuli was still managing somehow to keep in touch with my grandparents, and in fact visited them the night before they died....

While those last weeks in Vienna are very largely a blank, I remember that my mother tried very hard to prepare me for my new life in England, and gave me all the information at her disposal. While nothing could be arranged for my brother beforehand, I at least was taken care of, for I would be going to a Mrs. C. who had heard of me through Cousin Adolf. My mother

This photo, taken soon after my brother and I arrived in England, shows two waifs in greatcoats meant to last for an indefinite future.

was already in correspondence with her, knew that she had three daughters, and hoped that I would be a good girl there. I would be sent to school again, but all that my mother could tell me about English schools was that the girls there wore some kind of uniform, which was usually navy blue. Therefore, when my brother and I were taken to one of the good tailoring establishments in the Kärntnerstrasse to be measured for winter coats, his was ordered to be made in herring-bone tweed, while mine was of navy blue wool. I still have a photo, probably taken soon after our arrival in England, in which we two waifs appear very lost in these extra large great-coats which were intended to last us as long as possible. I also clearly recall that my poor mother made one attempt to prepare me for the onset of the menstrual cycle. However she was not very good at explaining this possibility, and I was so horrified when she mentioned the word "blood", that she had to drop the subject again very quickly.

The hoardings with their Nazi propaganda were still up all over Vienna, and consequently I learnt what had happened to Onkel Max and Onkel Martin. Jews, the news report claimed, had become fat and flabby, and therefore they needed re-training and athletic exercise. For this reason they were being taken to special camps where proper physical programmes had been set up for them. Despite my own lack of skill in this sphere, I approved of gymnastics – after all the Greeks were great athletes – but this particular piece of information sounded ominous, rather than convincing, and instinctively I refrained from repeating it at home. A few days later, I also discovered, but this via some kind of grapevine rather than through any public notices, that my parents should not attempt to smuggle anything valuable out with me, for if the German guards found something, such as diamonds hidden in coat linings and the like, then they would prevent not only me, but all the children on the train with me, from leaving the country. Such a risk was clearly not worth taking. I had already learnt that my own possessions would be severely restricted, and that I was limited to one large suitcase. Though Trude, my most favourite doll, could accompany me, sadly, my beloved Marianne could not. The little gold chain and heart-shaped locket with its blue enamel front and tiny diamond in the centre, which I wore almost all the time – a gift from some grateful patient – also would have to be left behind.

Neither Christmas 1938, nor the subsequent farewell visits to great-aunts and grandparents have left any tangible imprint on my mind. Undoubtedly they were much too painful to carry with me, and so my memory has blocked them out beyond recall. Shortly after New Year's, my parents were told that because I at least already had a guaranteed destination in England, the Quakers were prepared to accept my brother as well, and would find a suitable home for him on arrival; thanks to the good offices of Bloomsbury House which coordinated all transports, a train-load of children would be leaving immediately, and both of us could join that convoy. Our sturdy, dark-brown suitcases were closed, we struggled into our new coats, and I clutched Trude for security. Fräuli, who couldn't come to the train station with us when we left for Frankfurt, wasn't able to be with us this time either. Instead, my father seems to have accompanied us, for at the last minute he handed me a little silver marcasite cross and chain, with the assurance that this was something that I could safely take along. Presumably my mother was there as well, comforting my little brother; that last injunction, to look after him, must have come from her. All too soon the coach doors banged firmly shut and the guard blew his whistle. We choked and swallowed hard, but I don't think that we cried; we were too stunned.

For as long as we could see anything of the train station and of the mass of grown-ups left behind, we waved our handkerchiefs frantically out of the carriage windows. Then we started singing *Nun Ade du mein lieb Heimatland* ("Farewell to Thee, My Beloved Homeland"), one of many such songs in which wandering scholars and apprentices seeking their fortune in the wide world used to give vent to their home-sickness. In more recent times, these popular songs appealed to groups of young people on holiday, hiking beyond the borders of their own province or region, while primary schools found them useful for inculcating patriotic fervour; long ago, all of us had learnt them. Our singing began spontaneously, for the words seemed to express the sentiments appropriate to our present situation, but even before we had reached the second stanza – again spontaneously – our song died away. Its sentiments, after all, were *not* appropriate. Under the evil influence of Hitler, our homeland had disowned us; we were all keenly aware of this rejection, and realised that it was pointless to express love for a country which only wished to get rid of us as quickly as possible. Instead, though we had never met before, we chatted a little among ourselves, reassuring each other that we were taking nothing away with us that might cause trouble with the German guards.

Many hours later, the train stopped briefly in Frankfurt, and to my surprise, Onkel Max and Onkel Martin were at the station to greet us. They stood side by side in their dark suits and heavy overcoats, and despite their smiles, seemed strangely haggard. Somehow they did not look like themselves. When the train pulled out again, the uncles lifted their hats in a last salutation, and I realised with a sudden shock that their heads were shaven so that they looked almost bald. Obviously they had just been released from Buchenwald, the Concentration Camp in which they had been interned during the *Krystallnacht* round-up, for so far the Nazis were still playing a cat and mouse game with their victims, and many of those who had been arrested that night were shortly afterwards temporarily released. The fortunate few, like Onkel Max and Onkel Martin, who were able to use this respite to flee the country, later told of gas ovens, already then in the process of construction. Little as I knew of all this at the time, my uncles' strange appearance disturbed me profoundly and left a haunting memory.

As soon as we had crossed the border and arrived in Holland, the train stopped again. Now we were truly safe from the Nazis and need no longer worry about German soldiers holding us back from freedom. But relief was tinged with fear – all who were dear to us were still living amidst the danger from which we had just escaped! At the border station, a great many friendly Dutch women came up to the train, bringing mugs of hot chocolate, and tried to talk to us, presumably wishing to cheer us up, but despite our gratitude, we were unable to respond in any real way, for we could not understand them. Above all, we were emotionally exhausted, for already we longed for our families, and the strange language in which we were being greeted was the first concrete indication that we were irrevocably separated from them. By early evening we had reached the docks and were put into the ship that was to take us across the Channel. Just before embarking, we were given a light supper, but a number of children, including myself, were hardly able to eat anything, and so my brother could tuck into an extra large portion. The next morning, while climbing down from his bunk, past mine below, he became sea-sick, soiling my clothes as well as his own. Resentful of his greediness the night before, I was cross rather than sympathetic, and left it to an adult to clean us both up, before our journey continued on yet another train. Late on a bleak, wintry afternoon, we arrived at our final destination.

What happened once we reached Victoria Station is once again largely a blank. Suddenly I am waiting in some kind of sitting room – most likely at Bloomsbury House, which had become the headquarters of the Jewish *Kindertransport* organisation as well as the centre for all attempts to rescue children at risk, and in this capacity was also used by the English Quakers. My brother is no longer with me, but I have no idea when and how we became separated and clutch my doll tightly for reassurance. A strange lady approaches and addresses me, speaking a few broken German phrases in a very queer accent. I feel rather frightened of her, especially since she is wearing a bright red lipstick with nail varnish to match, and I am accustomed to neither one of these. In the Germany and Austria of my youth, even the most discreet use of make-up was practically unknown among the upper middle classes, and though I had frequently seen my mother in evening dress, even on such occasions she had never worn lipstick. Fräulein Else, who came every week to do my mother's nails, might have given them a coat of colourless varnish, but probably merely buffed them.

Bewildered but obedient, I go with Mrs. C., who has told me to call her "Aunt Evelyn". We journey by car and soon arrive at a strange house which seems very tall and narrow to me. Halfway up, I am greeted in French by a kindly, comfortable-looking governess who reminds me of my own nanny, and am told that she is called "Seb", which is really an abbreviation of "Mam'selle", and thus parallels the origin of my Fräuli's name. Seb takes me to the top of the house where a fair-haired girl, considerably taller than I, with rather high shoulders, greets me and asks "*Voulez-vous jouer?*" I try to show polite interest, and am rescued by Seb who insists on an early supper and bed. Before I know it, my first day in London has ended.

CHAPTER V
ANGLO-SAXON ATTITUDES

The first English sentence that I remember learning painfully goes as follows: "In ze park - we must - not put - Hans on - ze leash." These apparently simple words express a whole network of radical changes that made my life in England very different from anything that I had ever known before. To begin with, though my mother was very fond of animals, in our cramped quarters in Vienna it had obviously been impossible to keep any pets, and even in Velden we had never been exposed to any. Now I was discovering what a wonderful and exasperating companion a dog could be, for Hans, an elderly dachshund whom the family affectionately described as a sausage dog, knew every trick with which to take advantage of his position. When not indoors, he shared the small garden behind the house with a tortoise belonging to Julia, the youngest daughter of the family. Eventually, I too acquired such a pet, which I named "Sunshine", though the little creature could never take the place of the doll Trude in my affections. The tortoises spent their time hiding in the shrubbery, but Hans regularly came along when Julia and I accompanied Seb to Kensington Gardens, only a short distance from the house where we lived. Here another new experience awaited me, for in this park one was actually *invited* to walk and play on the grass, while dogs were allowed to run freely. Obviously I had found such a concept hard to believe, or the sentence about not putting Hans on the leash would not have had to be drilled into me so vigorously. Our walks were further enhanced by the fact that suddenly I was allowed to wear ordinary shoes outside, instead of laced boots, which in Vienna had been considered essential for my weak ankles. Soon the hated boots had disappeared altogether; and along with never having to put them on again came the strange experience of actually being asked each morning to choose what dress I wanted to wear that day!

While so much freedom was startling and needed getting used to, there were of course other, less positive adjustments, with which I had to cope. Most difficult of all was the constant sense of being beholden, and therefore of having no rights. Aunt Evelyn would have been horrified, of course, if she had known that I felt this way, and certainly did nothing that could encourage such sentiments. My adherence to the heroic code of the Greek epic,

however, as well as my recent experiences in Austria, combined
to make me very conscious of being dependent on strangers, an
object of charity, who could never take acceptance for granted.
For some time I even tried to suppress my appetite as far as
possible, but found such abstinence extremely difficult, since
English food was far less stodgy than what I was used to, and
hence never seemed to fill me in the same way. In particular,
toast at breakfast time seemed a poor substitute for the bread
which had been a staple part of my diet. There were also strange
new nursery rules that prevented one from any real indulgence –
you could put either jam on your bread, or butter, but *never* both.
In any case, jam belonged only to tea or to high tea, while in the
morning something peculiar called marmalade was brought to
the table. Honey, on the other hand, appeared both times though,
as with all other condiments, one was expected to take only a
single spoonful, putting it neatly on the side of one's plate;
spreading such a small amount on a piece of bread was very
different from pouring it freely all over, helping myself out of the
container, as I had been used to do at home. Somehow, in this
new setting, I never felt totally full, but it would have been
considered greedy to demand more than anyone else, and it seemed
to me that I had no right to ask for special consideration.

My sense of obligation might have been less pressing and
easier to bear if I had realised that the burden of my care did not
fall on one person alone, but that numerous people and organisations
had contributed to make my arrival and stay in Britain possible.
While the Quakers had arranged for my transport, and a Catholic
Committee dealing with refugee children had made itself
responsible for my schooling, various well-meaning individuals of
limited means were contributing small guaranteed monthly sums for
my keep; some forty years later, I found apologetic letters from a
number of them who could no longer meet this obligation once
war broke out. As a child, I knew nothing about all these
arrangements, which in any case eventually collapsed, leaving
me as dependent on the generosity of Mrs. C. as I had thought I
was from the beginning. At the time, the grandeur of the
establishment in which I was suddenly placed naturally led me to
assume that I owed everything to the family who lived there; and
through fear of presuming on this generosity, I often became
clumsy and awkward, qualities I had never shown at home.

Indeed, in comparison with our Viennese flat, the pre-war
household in Kensington was far more impressive. Although Seb

behaved very much like Fräuli, scolding and comforting in turn, she was really there to act as governess, rather than as a mere nanny, and was supposed to speak French with us most of the time. She herself came from Lausanne, which was said to have the purest French, but the naughty C. girls often ignored all her efforts and responded only in English. Seb was kind rather than firm, and could easily become flustered, at which times she broke into a peculiar mixture of French and English, which we enjoyed making her talk. Below the stairs was a cook named Mabel, as well as a parlourmaid called Emily, who in the afternoons appeared complete with lace apron and head-dress, and on Sundays assumed the responsibility of taking me along to Mass. My sensitivity to social nuances made me feel rather uncomfortable about these outings because I realised very quickly that going to church with this young Irish woman was somewhat *infra dig* and reflected badly on my own denominational affiliation. However, the subject of religion seemed to be as taboo here as it had been at home in Vienna, so I had to keep these disloyal ideas to myself. Besides, my faith was the one constant factor in a world which had turned upside down in every other way, and therefore I clung to it instinctively, even though this allegiance only accentuated how different I was from everyone else in the household.

Mrs. C., who was separated from her husband, valued learning, while her three daughters were artistically rather than academically inclined, and hence not at all like me. Rowena, the eldest and most talented, had almost completed her studies at Dartington, a boarding school which concentrated on the arts, where she had her own pony and was training to become a dancer. In all the time that I lived with the C. family, Rowena, whose glamour fascinated me, rarely came home, and then only for very brief visits, but nevertheless seemed to be close to her mother. I suspect that her two sisters, who attended a day school in London, envied her position and life style. Both of them seemed to detest their studies, and Gillian, the middle daughter, who was mildly interested in painting and was nearing the legal age for leaving school, could hardly wait to do so. The only part of school that Julia liked was acting; in fact, I can still repeat verbatim Marullus' passionate defence of Pompey which occurs in the first scene of *Julius Caesar* because shortly after my arrival, I heard it practised so incessantly at home. Julia, who was barely two years older than I, had obviously been bullied by her two older sisters, particularly by

Gillian, and now she meted the same treatment out to me. Having just embarked on adolescence, with a particularly difficult temperament, she was resentful of the world at large, but especially of me, who was close at hand, and of whom, inevitably, she felt extremely jealous. Not only was I totally unaware of this fact, but having never had any close contact with other girls, I also did not know how to enter into their world. Perhaps Julia had expected greater companionship and someone with whom she could share her secret thoughts, particularly as regards her appearance, and was disappointed that I was still such a child and cared so little about what I looked like. Nevertheless, she frequently requested my opinion as to what did or did not suit her, and I never knew what to say since I was not skilled in diplomacy, while an honest answer might well earn her wrath. Half the time I did not understand her, and the other half I felt that, given my subservient situation, I had no right to complain. Whenever any of this came to her notice, Seb would hasten to my defence like an anxious mother hen, while I tried to efface myself, since I could ill afford the luxury of vindicated righteousness, and felt already sufficiently singled out by being so different from the others. After all, my lack of English, my love of school, where I knew what was expected of me and felt far more comfortable than I did at home, even my complexion, proclaimed me to be a foreigner, a cuckoo in the nest. On top of all this, despite having spent so many summers at Velden, I had no real affinity for country life, whereas Gillian and Julia seemed passionately fond of it. Though some of their knowledge came from actual experience, their love of all dumb creatures owed as much to a mind-set formed by early acquaintance with the Peter Rabbit characters, and with such creatures as Toad of Toad Hall and Winnie the Pooh, none of whom I had ever encountered before; in place of dolls, the Kensington nursery was filled with stuffed animals.

Perhaps because she was a foreigner herself, Seb was more inclined to pity my condition and to make a special fuss over me, but Mrs. C. wanted me to be treated like a normal child and to be integrated into the family as quickly as possible, and therefore sent me to school right away. Since the Catholic Committee was willing to arrange payment of fees, I went to a nearby Ursuline convent school, having carefully memorised the one essential English sentence "I do not understand". The nuns were quite kind in a brisk, matter-of-fact way, and the girls did not tease me unduly, playing no worse tricks than trying to teach me unsuitable words which I refused to repeat, since their laughter made me guess that they were designed to shock our class mistress. I may even have picked up a little English in the short time that I was there – one day apparently, I came home from school, and when asked what I had eaten for lunch, replied that it had been "the husband of a cow"! Strange that I should know the word "husband" but not the word "beef"! I can also remember having to memorise a fairly long poem which began "We had a loving Mother once" and which went on to lament the fact that modern industrialised England no longer showed devotion to the Virgin Mary. I understood the gist of the poem, if not all the words, but quickly realised that my recital of this piece was not appreciated by the C. family which was only nominally Anglican and decidedly anti-clerical. Seb, a good Calvinist, was profoundly shocked by what I was learning, and in general worried about my immortal soul. Luckily she did not impart these feelings to me, and only many years later did I learn that Mrs. C., whose judgement Seb trusted, had needed to reassure her that the Almighty would find my faith as acceptable as her own.

My time at this first school ended fairly abruptly, for Seb reported to Aunt Evelyn that I seemed to come home almost every day in tears. Years later, through one of those inexplicable flashes of illumination which unearth a long suppressed memory, I suddenly realised what must have happened and solved the verbal riddle to which it was linked. During recess, the girls would chatter happily in the school playground, and though much of their conversation was about horseback riding, quite often they would also discuss the attacks by Irish terrorists which were suddenly springing up all over England. For in mid-January, a number of IRA bombs exploded as far apart as London, Manchester, Birmingham and Alnwick, while at the beginning of February, bombs had been planted in two London underground stations. Since I could not really follow what was being said, and knew nothing of the political situation which agitated my schoolmates, the word "Irish", and especially the term "IRA" sounded very much like "Aryan" to me. Understandably, I was extremely frightened and upset to be encountering this hateful word again, and remember sobbing "even here" as I walked home. Undoubtedly someone there tried to find out what was wrong with me, and though I might have complained in a vague way about the behaviour of the other girls, the truth appeared to be so dreadful that I was much too afraid to admit what was really the matter. So when Aunt Evelyn, who naturally assumed that my classmates were at fault, went to the headmistress and demanded an explanation, no very satisfactory answer was forthcoming. Based on concern for me and bolstered by ingrained English anti-Papist feelings, she informed the nuns that she had not rescued this child from the bullying of the Nazis to be bullied now by Catholic schoolgirls. Since she had promised to have me raised as a Roman Catholic, she agreed that I might continue with the private catechism classes which a German priest had been giving me at the convent school. However, she considered all other arrangements cancelled and removed me from the school, telling the nuns that she would pay the fees for my education herself in some smaller, more congenial institution.

Shortly thereafter I started attending "Miss Puttick's Children's Classes", a kind of advanced kindergarten cum primary school, held in a private house similar to the one in which I was living, and almost around the corner. All the instruction there was given by two or three female teachers, for as far as I can remember, the whole school contained only about fifteen children, split up into small groups, each one at work on a separate project. Since the average age of the boys and girls must have been around eight, I was probably the oldest child there, but I do not recall noticing this or feeling out of place. While indoors we wore flowered percale smocks, in soft pink, over our everyday clothes, when we were taken to Kensington Gardens to play rounders, a gentle version of baseball, we put on our green blazers which proudly bore the crest "MPCC". I have no recollection of how and when we studied any academic subject, but have happy memories of learning a little simple bookbinding by being shown how to fashion book covers and making marbled end pages. The latter process, which involved stirring a mixture of colours, was particularly fascinating because one could never foretell just what pattern would finally emerge. When we were satisfied with our handiwork and had dried the pages, our teacher showed us how to put them together to make attractive little booklets which we could then use as we pleased. Having poetry read aloud to us must also have formed part of the daily routine, since I remember that the rhythm and imagery of Blake's *The Tyger* had appealed to me so much that I wanted to copy this poem into my booklet, without noticing that actually I already knew it by heart. Thus, in Miss Puttick's little establishment, imperceptibly I began to acquire a basic knowledge of English, for it was a comfortable and safe environment in which to learn, where I was allowed to progress at my own speed, and where no one nagged me about my inability to produce a proper "th" or kept correcting all my other mispronunciations. This tended to happen a great deal in the C. household, doubtless with the best of intentions, though under so much critical appraisal I became extremely self-conscious, which only seemed to make matters worse.

Linguistic problems went hand in hand with physical ones. Although I had never been good at gymnastics, both swimming and skating had demanded a certain style and grace which I had been able to reach without too much difficulty. London in late winter and early Spring offered no opportunity for either sport, and instead, whenever Julia went to her ballet classes, I was taken along as well. Since this activity was entirely new to me and demanded skills closer akin to gymnastics, I could not follow the necessary movements and seemed very awkward to others, as well as to myself. Some time in early Spring, the class started practising a little playlet, a danced adaptation of some fairy tale, which was going to be presented to all interested parents. Feeling that something had to be done with this child who lagged behind everyone else, the ballet instructor made me the prince, hoping that this role would allow me to feel important, though in fact, I had nothing to do except to sit quite still in the centre, while all the action revolved around me. I was intelligent enough to realise that if the role of prince was some kind of prize, then it was really a booby prize, which got me conveniently out of the way. I did not resent such treatment because I knew that my clumsiness made any real participation impossible, and I did not want to spoil the play, but my self-confidence sank even lower. Soon I became as awkward at home as everyone there expected me to be, even though originally I had not shown any tendencies to spill or drop things unduly, and was not in the habit of bumping into furniture or knocking it over. In fact, shortly after my arrival in England, Aunt Evelyn had given an afternoon sherry party, and once the guests had been admitted by Emily, Julia and I, dressed in similar organdy frocks, and coached behind the door by Seb, had carried in trays and handed around drinks. These tasks I had managed without knocking into anyone or spilling any sherry, even though I was aware of being pointed out to Mrs. C.'s friends as the little refugee girl she had been expecting for so long. Continual reminders to be careful, however, acted like a self-fulfilling prophecy and thus the longer I stayed in England, the more self-conscious and clumsy I became, especially during those early months in London.

Can I trust these fragmentary memories which seem so real to me, when my diary focuses on quite different events? The all-too-few entries during that first year in England are written in an extremely neat German hand, except for the date which is superimposed in Roman script. The book opens with a single undated entry of January 1939 in which I talk to the diary as if it were a real person – in fact, this is what I actually claim it is for me – someone to whom I'll tell everything, all my deepest joys and griefs, while asking it to keep my secrets, and not to mind if I do not use it every day. These thoughts are expressed in the unaffected language of an eleven-year old, who concludes by saying, "I am going to try hard to have only good things to tell you". Then follow four dated entries, beginning with 1 February when I lament that I have lost the familiar name of "Liesl", suggesting that thereby I have really lost my identity, but nevertheless insist that I am seldom homesick. However, I admit that if I have seen anyone else crying, this sets me off, and then I weep secretly at night into my pillow. I am glad that I do not cry more often! Despite these natural sentiments, the literary note is already creeping in for the passage opens with a rhetorical exclamation:

> Liesl! But I no longer bear the name of Liesl. No, that happy, carefree time is past. Sometimes I would like to be a baby again, and then a moment later I am pleased to be almost grown-up...

The entry for the next day is such an obvious example of self-dramatisation, that I seem to remember dimly realising this myself in the very act of writing. The whole self-conscious literary effort, which covers a page in the diary, deserves being translated in full here:

> I would like to see St. Stephen's Cathedral. How can this be accomplished? When I look out of the window, I see a church steeple. But the surroundings are quite different. Well, then I'll breathe lightly on the window pane, and imagine that I am recognising St. Stephen's Cathedral through the mist. For a few minutes I remain in my corner. Then the call "Elisabeth" startles me out of my dreams, and with a last melancholy look out of the window I return to reality.

The entries for 3 and 4 February, which concern my brother George, are hardly more down to earth. The Quakers had kept their promise to look after him, and since numerous families had offered to take in the refugee children they had evacuated, as soon as he arrived in London, the ideal home had been found for

This page, with its neat German script, is the first proper entry in my diary. The recent upheavals probably account for the fact that I dated it 1938 instead of 1939.

my brother up north, in Kirkby Stephen. There he was staying with a childless schoolmaster and his wife who doted on this clever little boy who learned so readily and clearly shared their scientific and musical interests. Mrs. C., however, decided that he was much too far away from me, and that being an only child could not be good for him. The couple up north were heart-broken and protested at this unnecessary separation, but my foster-mother was a forceful personality and adamantly insisted that different arrangements had to be made. Consequently, just when he had settled down in Kirkby Stephen, my poor brother was now being uprooted again,

to join the H. family. The latter had six children and lived on a
farm near Petersfield, Hants, in a far less grand style than Mrs.
C. George was to stay with us overnight in London, before being
taken there. My diary shows that I am wildly excited at the
prospect of seeing him again, for I write,

> I am happy about the answer, 'Yes, twenty minutes past five'. I
> am so happy that I have a brother who will come this afternoon.
> Only now do I realise what love between brother and sister mean.
> Love of my mother, long-standing love for Fräuli, these endure,
> but love that children have for one another at school has already
> often disappointed me for usually it passes as quickly as the rose
> which fades away, but not the love between brother and sister...

My diary entry for the following day describes how cute the little
chap looked when he arrived wearing such a big cap, and how
much he had to tell. It fails to mention that he rushed straight to
the piano and started playing, without even taking his wool gloves
off or asking for permission; and that he also manifested his
frustrations by kicking poor Hans. Apparently I kept hovering
around him, apologising for whatever he was doing, though Aunt
Evelyn, who had no experience with little boys and distrusted
them, thought that he was badly spoiled and did not hold me
responsible for his reprehensible behaviour. All this I was told
years later. The diary entry only records that in the morning
George came along to my second dancing lesson, and that
afterwards he was allowed to display his musical talents on the
piano there. Admiring his performance with sisterly pride, I note
with a fine literary flourish, "How sprightly the little brown fingers
swept across the keys!" The visit to the dance studio was followed
by our going for confession to the German priest who was giving
me catechism lessons. In the afternoon, we were planning to feed
the birds and to show George a little bit of London. The last
sentence comments "How painful I will find this separation."

There are no further entries for the year 1939, though why
this should be so I do not know. However 1 January 1940 begins
with nine pages which try to fill in some of the blanks, since they
attempt an overview of the past year and are entitled "Memories".
Although still written in German script, except for the date and
the title, the handwriting here is already no longer as tidy as it
used to be. I begin by saying that much has changed since I last
wrote in my diary, but then, making an obvious effort to pick up
where I had left off, go on to describe how unhappy my brother
was at first in his new home, and that I had to tell Julia's mother

about it; later on, however, he seemed to settle down. The diary does not record a rather pathetic and at the same time amusing detail: in his first letter after moving to Petersfield, George complained bitterly that the H. family gave him only one face cloth with which he was expected to wash all of himself, enumerating each bodily part that had to be dealt with in this way, while reminding me that in Austria we had always been expected to use two flannels, one for our face, and a second for the rest of our body. Angrily exaggerating, he claimed to have caught whooping cough and an enormous cold because all the rooms were so chilly, and rejected my attempts to encourage him, declaring firmly: "Altogether, it isn't nice here. So you see, you were quite wrong about what you said in your letter." At least one of George's problems was solved when Aunt Evelyn purchased a sponge which I was allowed to send him. Remembering all my concern about my brother leads me on to admit, "I believe that at the time I took things much too seriously", but then, to illustrate such misplaced seriousness, I mention that I had a long discussion with Seb as to whether or not I wanted a new doll.

Though the paragraph continues without pause, I have obviously turned to a new topic with the startling sentence, "By now I hate Julia", remembering the occasion when Aunt Evelyn was trying to teach me dancing, and Julia attempted to put a stop to this by whispering that I should not be bothering her mother who was really much too tired. Julia has done things like that very often since, I complain, because she takes pleasure in intimidating others, and is a real bully, giving unkindness directed only at me a wider significance, and clearly failing to recognise the underlying jealousy. Instead, the diary assumes that Julia has learnt such behaviour from Gillian, which suggests that I am remembering the many squabbles between them that I had noticed soon after my arrival in England. At this point my entry also expresses disgust with Julia's troublesome vanity, for amidst much else, "every other day she washes her hair, and never leaves me in peace, asking me if she looks beautiful or not, and at night she turns on the light again especially in order to look at herself in the mirror". However, blaming Julia's treatment of me on how she herself used to be treated by Gillian leads to the puzzling question as to where Gillian herself had learnt to be so overbearing. What makes Gillian behave like that, the diary asks plaintively, going on to express the certainty that Rowena, the eldest girl in the family, is quite different and would never have treated *her* younger sister in such a way!

In connection with the above, I also note that Tante Trudi (who together with Onkel Max had stopped briefly in England on her way to Chile) came to visit me in London towards the end of March and that I was terribly happy to see her. "I only told Tante Trudi that Julia behaved towards me a little bit the way I used to behave towards George" I admit in the diary. Obviously my aunt had wondered how well I was getting along with my foster sisters, and since I did not want to distress her, I had deliberately understated the situation. But what did I mean when I wrote "Later on I told her a big secret, and she told me one too"? Whatever confidences we exchanged, when she left again I was very upset, for I confess that I cried a great deal and longed for someone who could help me. My tears flow with renewed vigour on my mother's birthday, 19 September, when I think a lot about her, and about Vienna, as well as about Velden and Frankfurt. What the diary does not note, but what I can still remember, is that when I was already in bed that evening, Aunt Evelyn came into my room with her own glass of sherry, bringing along a small amount for me, and saying "We must toast your mother's birthday". It was the first time that I had ever tasted alcohol, and I did not care for it very much.

By the time this lengthy diary entry was being composed, we were no longer in London, but were living in Buckinghamshire, in the C. cottage called "Woodlands", not far from High Wycombe and Henley-on-Thames. Initially we had only gone there for the summer, but when war broke out in September, Aunt Evelyn did not want us to return to London. Hence Julia and I became day students at a nearby boarding school, while Gillian joined the land army and worked on local farms. This new location explains in part why so much of "Memories" is concerned with my religious obligations and the isolation I am experiencing. But perhaps some of this should be quoted directly:

> Since we have come to live here in the country, I can't even get to church anymore, because Emily is not here, and there is no Catholic church nearby. I never liked the church which I attended in London; it was too big and stately. I love a small, quiet, familiar little church, where there aren't too many people and where, at a small side altar, one can pour out one's heart. Since I don't go any longer to the convent school, I haven't had any religious instruction – I only have two simple prayerbooks – no German Bible – and English

writers like Scott and Merriman are very opposed to Catholicism
because it is the period of the Reformers, and so I am becoming
completely confused, and pray my Rosary less devoutly every day.

The heroic code seems to have given way to the romantic one
here, probably as the result of my current reading! How else can
I explain this sudden longing to pray in a little church with dim
religious light, considering that all the religious edifices I had
ever encountered in Vienna were just as "big and stately" as the
London church I now professed to dislike? While the diary entry
accurately reflects how alone and bewildered I felt at
"Woodlands", it also shows that I had forgotten much of my earlier
life in London, and suggests that my present state of mind might
be responsible for distorting some of these memories. This last
point is exemplified by my complaint that once I had been taken
out of that first convent school, my religious instruction had
instantly ceased, though nothing could be further from the truth.
After all, Mrs. C. had told the nuns that I would still come for my
regular German catechism lessons and that these had continued
for as long as possible is proven by a goodbye present from Pater
W.S., the priest who had instructed me. The interesting adult book
which he gave me and which I treasure to this day, is the
autobiography of a Dutch Benedictine monk, and bears an
inscription, dated 9 April 1939, urging me never to forget God
and to remain always a loyal daughter of the Roman Catholic
Church. To the best of her ability then, Aunt Evelyn had kept her
promise to my mother that I would be raised in my faith, and it
was Hitler who ended the catechism lessons when he recalled the
young priest to Germany in the Spring of 1939. Now I was totally
on my own, and though I had long been used to encountering
religious indifference, I felt bewildered by my first experience of
differing viewpoints and diverse religious prejudices, and missed
a trusty guide to help me sort out my ideas. Sir Walter Scott, all
of whose historical novels I was rapidly devouring, had obviously
confused me badly, as my reference to "the period of the
Reformers" indicates. The clumsy wording – showing that I am
losing facility in German – is not entirely clear, and may indicate
that the novels I am currently reading deal with this period.
However, it also suggests that even if I knew that the Reformation
had started in the sixteenth century, as far as I was concerned,
that movement was still in process here, and accounted for the
anti-Catholicism I encountered in English novelists. Yet much as
I disliked Scott's attitude to my Church, I loved all his books, for

I was becoming steeped in romantic history. So as a good Catholic, should I really be reading such novels, and would it be better if I did not do so? My conscience was not totally easy on that point, but there was no one whom I could ask for advice.

Obviously the diary entry has moved from an overview of the past into the present, because during that first school term in London, my limited English would not have allowed me to read any Scott novel, and I could only have started doing so quite recently at the new school which I had now been attending for almost four months. The dash which precedes the next sentence indicates that I am aware of this shift in time, and am once again returning to the past:

> I was taken out of the convent school because I had complained a number of times about the behaviour of the children. I have a vague idea that it was also because the school was too expensive. [Little did I realise that quite the reverse was true.] In any case, Aunt Evelyn wanted to make me happy and the second school to which I went was very small and I didn't like it very much. The children weren't especially nice, the mean children played tricks on the teacher, and one could learn very little. But really I was only there to improve my English, which indeed happened, and I learnt about famous painters, about Chaucer, and how one binds books. And I could practise my favourite sport - swimming. [Something which I had totally forgotten!] So to a certain extent, I learnt to like the school, and I was very sad when I had to leave it. Now I realise that it was my own fault, that I didn't always understand the children. [We seem to have got back to the convent school with this interesting comment which shows some awareness of a suppressed memory.] I will never forget one French nun. Her face seemed to me to be that of an angel, her voice was sweet and deep.

After several dashes, indicating that I am no longer looking back to the past, early adolescence manifests itself and I voice quite different concerns. I feel that I have changed a great deal and admit that I am growing a little vain, mentioning that I am trying hard to be graceful, and making the curious claim that sometimes my movements display a singular pride. I don't read any more stupid stories, [one wonders what these might have been?] but instead old-fashioned, famous and romantic novels, which I love. Aunt Evelyn says that I was much more clumsy when I first came – a comment which suggests not only that our country existence, as compared to London, was a little more relaxed, but also that the new school was helping me to gain self-confidence. Rowena, I note gratefully, has given me help and stimulation in my ideas regarding life, and to some degree I have been able to hold on to her encouragement. Years later, Aunt Evelyn told me that after talking long and earnestly to Rowena on one of her brief visits, I came to her later and said with great satisfaction, *"Now* I know what life is". The diary entry ends with the assertion that I am still hoping that my parents will be able to go to America. . . .

CHAPTER VI
THE PHONEY WAR

While the diary entry which concluded the previous chapter kept alternating between past and present, and carried me briefly forward to the beginning of 1940, it left out a good deal of 1939 that can be filled in from other sources. My first few months in London were made easier by the fact that on Sunday afternoons I was frequently allowed to visit elderly family friends who had left Austria many years before and were comfortably ensconced in Putney. Long ago they had briefly returned to Vienna, so I already knew them; now, in their spacious flat all was familiar to me – furniture and food, language and culture – and there were sometimes even letters from home. However, as in Austria, so here too, once the school year was over, we moved to the country, and soon I lost all contact with this last link to my childhood. Yet in a setting where the sun never stopped shining, while time seemed to stand still, I was scarcely aware of my loss. Indeed, the summer of 1939 was exceptionally fine, and the glorious weather formed a strange contrast to the growing international tensions of which even we children could not help but be aware, though I at any rate, at first paid little heed. More than anything, I hoped that moving to the country would allow me to go swimming again outdoors, though when I finally did, this proved disappointing in many ways. Compared to the warm lake at Velden, the Thames seemed surprisingly cold, and in any case, I was unable to swim there every day, since we lived at some distance from the river, and could only reach it by car. The infrequent expeditions, which always concentrated on first finding some suitable spot for a picnic, limited my time in the water, and instead of being able to show off my prowess, I found no one particularly interested in the sport, while my own skill, what with lack of practice and cold, seemed to be declining.

The so called "cottage" in which we lived was really a solid, two-storey farm house. However, it was not as spacious as the C. town house, and even though Emily never accompanied us here but went home for the summer, we were still somewhat crowded, especially when visitors came to stay. Because fewer bedrooms were available, and one extra child had to be accommodated, Julia was forced to move in with Gillian, while I, who had previously shared the old nursery with her, now slept in Seb's bedroom. These arrangements must have been difficult for Seb and for Gillian, both of whom lost their privacy, even if Seb who was easy-going and liked me, did not really object to my presence; as for me, I suddenly enjoyed far more peace and quiet than I had ever known before. Julia, on the other hand, could no longer boss me around so much, and instead, had to knuckle under to Gillian, a fact which I duly noted in my diary, considering it just retribution. Undoubtedly neither sister really liked sharing a room, but though they grumbled, they made the best of a situation which was considered to be merely temporary; after all, once they went back to London, the old order would be restored! Later on, when our summer arrangements turned out to be far more permanent than anyone had expected, various difficulties could be blamed on the war and would become part of doing one's bit.

I was already familiar with the cottage before we went to stay there for the summer months because we had visited it a few times in the Spring and during the Easter holidays, when we had gathered cowslips in the nearby meadows and bluebells in the woods. One could pick a whole armful and still not cause the slightest rift in the endless carpet spread before one's eyes, one of a greeny-yellow colour, the other a hazy mist of blue. For the first time too, I had come into real contact with country life when Julia had taken me to a small pond not too far from the cottage, which had been covered with greenish scum that after a while had miraculously turned into tadpoles. I had helped Julia to carry some of these home in old jam jars and had watched them grow into small frogs, returning them a few days later to their native habitat. Now that we were here for a much longer stay, Julia could keep guinea-pigs, who tended to multiply quite frequently, though each pregnancy caused considerable excitement and worry because occasionally the females became impregnated far too young, with disastrous consequences. To please Julia, I sometimes visited her pets in their hutches, and duly admired them, but never had the slightest desire to own any of my own. Nevertheless, soon I too had to assume responsibility for a domesticated rodent, for on one of his rare visits that summer, Cousin Adolf suddenly arrived with two rabbits – a black one for Julia and a white one for me. I named mine Hilda, an approximation of my mother's name, but paid little attention to the poor creature, and the rabbit reciprocated such lack of affection by becoming bad-tempered, with a tendency to bite. I have no recollection of what happened to Hilda, so probably she did not last very long in my care.

The back of the cottage faced a small courtyard around which clustered a number of low buildings originally intended for farming use – a cool shed for churning butter, and barns for milking and the like. Adjoining the house was a garden with vegetables, flowers and a few fruit trees; later on, as part of the war effort, Mrs. C. rented an additional plot across the road, so that we might become self-sufficient and grow all our own vegetables. Even before we had this extra land at our disposal, Julia and I were encouraged to plant and grow something of our own choosing. Julia knew rather better than I what to do, though I do not remember what she produced, whereas the packet of radish seed which I had purchased did not fare very well. Once the seeds actually sprouted and started to grow, I was so delighted by this process that despite warnings that radishes could become too large, I refused to pull them out of the ground. Eventually my radishes, of which I had been so proud, proved to be wooden and totally inedible, and the experiment of growing something on my own was never repeated. On a more practical level, Julia and I were expected to do a certain amount of weeding which neither of us enjoyed, and we were also encouraged to pick the mushrooms in an adjacent field. These seemed to spring up miraculously overnight amidst the cow patties, but one had to be out so early to collect them before anyone else got there first, that we usually left this task to Gillian. It was far more pleasant to go out a little later and to meander up and down our little road, looking for the sweet wild strawberries that seemed to thrive among the hedgerows on either side. On my first forays, I was primarily interested in eating them myself, but when I discovered that Julia was leaving the strawberries on their long stems and tying them into little bunches to place on her mother's breakfast tray, I readily followed her example. Not only did English schoolgirl parlance describe such an act as "being a copycat", behaviour considered thoroughly despicable, but as far as Julia was concerned, I seemed to be trying to worm my way into her mother's affections – hence the resentment and annoyance which she so often felt towards me, and which I can understand much better today! Towards the end of the summer we all pitched in to help neighbours who had numerous large, old fruit trees, though our limited assistance may not have been really required, and was merely an excuse for sending us home with heaping baskets. I still recall a summer harvest – was it 1939 or 1940, or possibly both? – which provided us with an overabundance of greengages, yellowish-green plums which were sweeter and juicier than any fruit I have encountered since. Later on, in early autumn, we beat the bushes in the nearby woods, to gather hazel nuts.

As long as we were still finishing our school term in London, we children had not paid a great deal of attention to the war clouds gathering all around us, though throughout that Spring, Hitler continued to flex his muscles, encouraged by Neville Chamberlain's Munich agreement back in the autumn of 1938, with its policy of appeasement at any price. By mid-March of 1939 the Nazis had annexed Czechoslovakia, and there were already early signs that they intended to invade Poland. At the end of March, Britain and France confirmed their pledge to defend Poland, but since they had abandoned Czechoslovakia to its fate, were they really going to take a stand this time? And was there any guarantee that Hitler would stop with Poland? Her memories of the First World War, coupled with an instinctive distrust of all Germans, convinced Aunt Evelyn that war was bound to come soon, and like a growing number of Britons, she felt that it would be better to get it over with, rather than to offer endless concessions. When we went to the country at the beginning of the summer, she was already anticipating that we might not be returning to London in September and made sure that the cottage had alternate means of cooking and heating available, and that there was a large supply of candles and oil lamps on hand. Now that we were at "Woodlands", even before the official outbreak of war we became accustomed to gathering around the wireless, as it was then called, for the daily evening news. June and July brought more IRA bombs, as well as belligerent rumblings from Churchill, and a gearing up in the production of armaments and the construction of air raid shelters to withstand the expected attack. When in August, instead of joining Churchill's proposed military alliance, Russia shocked Britain by signing a non-aggression pact with Germany, in preparation for carving up Poland between them, the British forces were finally mobilized and the evacuation of children from vulnerable English cities began. Julia and I were out on the lawn on 3 September, a lovely summer day, playing with our rabbits and allowing them to nibble the fresh grass, when the tired voice of Neville Chamberlain came over the air, declaring that we were at war.

Emily, who had gone back to Ireland for the summer, was now definitely not returning to England, and Mabel, the cook, soon left us as well, so that Aunt Evelyn and Seb had to take over in the small kitchen. Paradoxically, our meals did not suffer from

Mabel's departure, but in fact improved a great deal, especially the vegetables. Gillian too, did some light cooking and began to assume increasing responsibility in the house; given Seb's inability to exercise firm control, quite often when her mother was absent, she had to take charge and tell Julia and me what to do. As far as our official household chores were concerned, we were expected to tidy up after ourselves and to help with the general washing up, leaving the heavy pots and pans for Gillian or for Seb. In the outside world too, many changes were taking place which soon affected us, especially the introduction of the blackout. This practice had to be carefully observed, and it required much ingenuity and sewing, mostly done by Seb, to transform enough heavy material into suitable curtains for every window in the house. As soon as it grew dusk, one had to make sure that not a single chink of light was showing anywhere, in case a German plane might be inadvertently helped. Along with the blackout came petrol rationing which started less than three weeks after Mr. Chamberlain's announcement.

Since she was determined to leave school, and had at least completed her intermediate certificate, Gillian was using the summer of 1939 to discover if her talents sufficed for the career she really wanted. Consequently much of her time was spent practising what her weekly lessons with a local artist had taught her about the use of oil colours, and one could often see her heading towards the woods with her easel and box of paints. However, all this came to an abrupt end because after the outbreak of hostilities, girls of Gillian's age were expected to be back in school or else engaged in some activity which would benefit the war effort. After much pleading with her mother, she was allowed to join the land army and seemed to enjoy her outdoor work much more than ever she had her academic studies. Julia and I, of course, had to return to classes, and this time we both attended the same school, though Julia was ahead of me by about two forms. This boarding school, in which we were day pupils, was run along highly idiosyncratic lines, but despite its various oddities, provided an excellent education. I remember my time there as very happy, and wrote in my diary on the first of January 1940, "My new school is big and full of freedom, and I love it there". The Garden School, as it was called, has long since ceased to exist; if I were to go back to it today, no doubt it would not be nearly as "big" as I thought it then. Once upon a time, the main building had been the stately home which some Eastern potentate had built for himself in

England; it now contained the dormitories as well as the dining room where I, a day pupil, would join the boarders for lunch. Our classes were held around a courtyard, supposedly in quarters which had once been the stables of the property. I cannot tell today whether any of this history is factually accurate; it is certainly what we schoolgirls assumed to be the truth. The grounds were large and included a swimming pool as well as playing fields; in the former, I was taught rudimentary life-saving, while my favourite game on the latter was field hockey. The main building also contained the headmistress' office, where I was given private elocution lessons to help improve my English pronunciation, and a large assembly-hall in which we gathered every morning to start the day with an inspirational address, often related to the school motto which was "Obey the Highest: Love the Best", followed by a hymn and prayer, and relevant announcements.

Essentially geared to be a boarding school, and containing a number of pupils whose families lived far away, The Garden School tried to accommodate all its members and though Anglican in tone, did its best to be non-denominational. Consequently specific Christian references were carefully omitted from our morning hymn so that, for example, we often pleaded for those in peril on the sea with the well-known words, *Eternal Father, Strong to Save*, but did not sing the stanza which refers to Christ walking on the waves and calming the storm. Because of wartime conditions, Julia and I were allowed to attend as day students, and were not required to purchase the dark green uniform which all the other girls wore. Similarly, though this was an institution limited to girls, one or two little boys had been admitted into the lowest form, which was known as "The Busy Bees". My form was called "The Pillars". Along with this odd nomenclature, almost every member of staff had her own nickname, beginning with the headmistress, who was called "Owaissa", which was supposed to translate into something like "Big Chief". My instructor in Latin and Maths was referred to as "Toots", an abbreviation of her real name, while the mistress for English and History was known as "Brittain", which was actually her family name. All of them were excellent teachers, able to give personal attention to each child in their small classes, and except for French grammar, which I found rather boring, I enjoyed every subject. In addition to purely academic work, we played all the usual sports; spent time at arts and crafts, where I worked with leather and with clay, and even learnt how to make a dress; practised

In my first term at the Garden School, we studied the Reformation. Given my
own situation, quite unconsciously I identified with the unfortunate monks.

singing, which taught us many traditional English folk songs;
and were introduced to something called Greek dancing as well
as to a form of movement known as "Dalcroze Eurhythmics".
For the latter we were required to wear a lovely deep-blue, silky
tunic and soft, flat suede sandals. I can recall putting my name
down for the purchase of these requisite sandals without checking
at home first, and then being very frightened by my presumption;
perhaps I even received a scolding from Seb.

Our interest in academic subjects was stimulated by
imaginative means. We learned a considerable amount of Latin,
for instance, through putting on a simplified version of Plautus'
Miles Gloriosus, and thoroughly enjoyed ourselves acting out
this brief comedy. In our history workbooks we could illustrate
the notes which we had taken in class with relevant drawings and
paintings of our own choosing. Among the many I produced, there
is one showing gory flames as Mary Tudor burns a Protestant at
the stake. The colours of the burning flames, like those of the
earlier setting sun, no doubt appealed to me, though my choice of
subject matter seemed wrong for a Roman Catholic and left me
feeling uneasy. On the other hand, we carried on a very lively
and formal debate on the subject of "Was Elizabeth's Treatment
of Mary Stuart Justified?", and here I had no twinges of conscience
over taking Mary's side. Not only is this particular event illustrated

The next term brought us to the Reign of Mary Tudor. Despite pangs of conscience, I could not help enjoying lurid scenes.

in my workbook, but the whole episode also remains engraven in my memory because of an unfortunate accident caused by the rearrangement of the furnishings to create adequate space for the orators. When everything had been pushed to the side, and one of the chairs had actually been placed on top of a table, I chose to climb up there, ostensibly so as to get out of the way, but actually because I rather enjoyed my lofty perch. In the excitement over the argument, however, I fell off the chair and landed very hard on the concrete floor. Though my back hurt badly, after a little while I was able to get up and make light of the pain, which caused a girl named Daphne W., whom I secretly admired because she was so much better than I at sports, to praise me for being so brave. I wanted to keep her golden opinion of me and hated being sent home, but once there, I had to admit how much it hurt and Seb put me to bed. In Vienna, I would have been rushed to Dr. Gersuni, our paediatrician, who doubtless would have ordered the necessary x-rays right away. This was war-time Britain, however, deep in the country, and anyhow, the C. family who had their own trusted G.P. in London, did not believe that every ache and pain required immediate medical attention the way my own parents did. Nevertheless, after remaining in bed for a couple of days, I was threatened with a visit to the doctor, an experience which I wanted to avoid at all costs, and therefore, despite residual pain, I got up and returned to school. In time the pain disappeared altogether, but the back troubles from which I suffered years later probably owe something to this fall.

Besides the multi-talented Daphne, who was so good at sports, only one other girl my own age sticks in my memory, though I have long forgotten her name. She too was a refugee child, either Austrian or German, though oddly enough, we never exchanged experiences or attempted to speak to each other in our mother tongue; in fact we had very little to do with one another. Prominent among the big girls was Leslie Hutchison, daughter of a popular black American crooner called "Hutch", probably the first Negro whom I had ever met, and an excellent athlete. Two other older girls also come to mind – one of them, who was German, caused a stir among us because she was briefly interned when all enemy aliens were rounded up; however in a very short time she was allowed to return to school. The other was a Catholic girl named Jean B., with whom I was occasionally permitted to go to church on Sunday. Jean would cycle over from school before breakfast, and would meet me near "Woodlands". From there we would walk together to a small make-shift chapel, scarcely speaking along the way, though I was always somewhat disappointed by her unresponsiveness to my conversational overtures. Perhaps Jean, a boarder at school, was glad to have a little quiet times to herself, perhaps she simply considered me a nuisance, since I neither possessed a bicycle nor knew how to ride one, and hence slowed her down considerably; whatever the reason, she appeared to consider me a liability rather than an ally from her own denominational camp, and made no attempt to be friendly. The building which was loaned to us for our worship lacked any kind of religious atmosphere, and as soon as the brief liturgy was over, we all scattered again. While such a Sunday ritual hardly gave one any sense of being part of a Catholic community, I was pleased that at least I could fulfill my obligations regarding Sunday Mass there, considering how often I had absolutely no opportunity to do so. One other obligation, that of abstinence from meat on Friday, proved easier to fulfill because the school served two sorts of dishes, one regular and the other for vegetarians. On Fridays, my lunch always came from the latter menu, and I rather wished that it could do so all the time because the vegetarian meals were far better prepared and more filling than the usual overcooked vegetables and meat which were the standard fare.

2 January 1940 contains a rather brief but important entry in my diary. The German has a somewhat literary and formal ring, as if I felt that this was the appropriate reaction to express:

> How happy I am today, how happy! These are the best news that I have had in years. They will travel on the third of January from Trieste to the U.S.A. [This sentence stands out because it is written in the Latin alphabet.] My entire life has been changed by war and I had given up the hope of ever seeing them again, but God willed otherwise. And I hope that soon I will be together with my parents again.

Clearly I was relieved to learn that my parents would really be safe soon, since there had already been several false starts earlier. At one point it had seemed likely that they would be able to emigrate to Latin America, and Aunt Evelyn had immediately started to prepare me for Spanish lessons. Though this scheme came to nothing, shortly thereafter my father was offered the position of doctor to a Christian mission in India. Plans for the long journey were already under way when Britain declared war on Germany and since India was still part of the Empire, my parents could no longer obtain an exit visa for what had suddenly become enemy territory. There was now very little time left, for no one knew how soon the U.S., whose sympathies lay with the allies, might become *persona non grata* in German eyes, while Italy seemed poised to enter the war at any moment, though on which side was still not quite certain. Given this situation, my parents managed to leave Austria in the nick of time. Even if their safety was very much on my mind, I had no real desire to join them, for the United States seemed terribly far away, and I was very happy in my English school. Hence my pious desire to be reunited soon with my parents was suitably expressed for my own edification rather than with any real wish that it might happen immediately.

After the above entry there is another long blank, and I do not resume writing until the Spring of 1940. By this time we were spending all our evenings knitting for the forces, while Gillian and Aunt Evelyn took turns reading aloud – a practice that had already begun in late autumn. The anti-aircraft gunners needed balaclava helmets and gloves which left the tips of the fingers free, and so were only completed to the first knuckle; the navy required stockings made of unprocessed, waterproof wool which smelled of sheep and had a strange texture; and for a while we also knitted white garments that would not show up against the snow, supporting the brave Finns who were fighting the Russians.

Seb and I knitted the European way, without even having to look,
and I was glad that I had been taught so well in Vienna, and now
could do something really useful. Along with knitting, rationing
was becoming part of our daily lives; it had already started in
early January with butter, sugar and bacon becoming only
obtainable for coupons. Living in the country, one noticed it
somewhat less, though in time even we children, who did not do
any grocery shopping, began to be aware of it.

Since this stretch of my diary is so fragmentary, some of the
chronological blanks can be filled by what The Garden School
had to say about my first term there. Presumably, this lasted from
approximately mid-September to shortly before Christmas 1939,
but cannot be dated precisely because according to the
idiosyncratic system of the school, only the opening and closing
dates for the *next* term are given in each report. This information
appears on the covering page of a little booklet, but without any
reference as to the specific year, and is then followed by the
undated signature of the headmistress, for once using her real
name. While the complete report would be worth quoting in full,
unfortunately that would take up too much space, since we were
not merely assigned numerical grades, and in fact, these were
never used. Instead, the rest of the booklet consists of individual
6"x 4" pages, later bound together, on which the relevant mistress
would carefully describe in a small, neat hand the content covered
each term by a particular subject, as well as the child's progress,
strengths and weaknesses. Parents or guardians would receive
three of these detailed reports each year.

To begin with, our form mistress who had general
responsibility for us "Pillars", and whom we called "Lois",
presents a "General Report" in which she notes that I settled
down quickly and happily, and that my enthusiasm and
perseverance in every subject enabled me to make satisfactory
all-round improvement. Amidst other comments, she writes,
"[Elisabeth] shows special aptitude for academic subjects and
we can no doubt expect to see still further progress when her
knowledge of English has increased... We shall hope to see further
development along other lines such as creative work and physical
activities, when these have ceased to be such new experiences
for her." After noting that I proved to be a stimulating and
cooperative member among the whole group, the last paragraph
of the General Report reads,

> Her performance in the end of term recitals was good and she was
> responsible for the preparation of her own speech on the comparison
> of Austrian and English schools.

It would be interesting to know how I compared the two school
systems! Though my own performance has totally faded from my
mind, I do remember a little about these end of term recitations in
which every pupil, with the possible exception of the "tinies"
had to take part. Depending on what form we were in, we presented
our speech before the assembled junior or senior division, which
suggests that the school must have been quite small, since
otherwise this training in public speaking would have consumed
far too much time. Lois also taught us French and noted that I
had a good foundation both in written and in spoken French. She
reports that during the term we worked on reading, dictation,
grammar and oral composition, and in addition produced a small
play and memorised some poetry and a song. My compositions
tend to be of a higher standard than my exercises and formal
grammar – though she did not know that I found these boring –
but I try hard and respond well to criticism. My enthusiasm is
stimulating for the whole class, but shouldn't lead me to push
ahead of my turn to get corrections and explanations. Obviously,
this "eager beaver" side of my character might sometimes have
manifested itself at home as well, and must have been particularly
irritating to Julia.

Brittain, writing about my work in English, notes at the outset
that I am "a very neat and tidy worker" – obviously part of my
Austrian training. My compositions on narrative, descriptive and
imaginative subjects show ability, though I am hampered by lack
of vocabulary. She describes the various grammatical and
structural problems we studied that term, and these seem
incredibly advanced by the standards of today. The final paragraph
shows what the school expected of eleven and twelve year olds:

> For literature we read some essays by modern and earlier essayists
> and "Much Ado About Nothing". Elisabeth showed a quick
> understanding of both play and essays and entered with zest into
> the reading of the parts.

Brittain also taught us history, which that term involved the Tudor
period and the political and social changes that the Reformation
caused in England and in the rest of Europe. She comments that I
am a delightful pupil to teach because I am so enthusiastic and
eager to learn, that I prepare well and take good notes (she kindly

refrains from saying anything about my erratic English spelling, which at this point occasionally still depends somewhat on German phonemes). Given my imagination, I should be able to produce interesting results in my illustrative work – clearly the burning of the heretics had not yet occurred!

Toots writes somewhat more briefly but equally positively about my work in Latin and Mathematics. Along with everyone else in my form, I was starting Latin from scratch and so had no problems whatsoever. Mathematics proved a little more difficult. As Toots says:

... She has an enquiring mind, eager to understand underlying principles as well as methods, and she works carefully on each new study. An unsettled school career hitherto has undoubtedly been detrimental to her standard, and again, this term it was necessary to spend some little time discovering her whereabouts in mathematics, but she has now made considerable headway and she is progressing smoothly.

Geography and Science were both taught by the same mistress, one E.M.H. Our work in Geography that term was devoted to studying South America. Here too I made satisfactory progress and my written exercises were always good, the report says. But I had trouble drawing maps and although I showed some improvement, still lacked clarity of detail and neatness. In Science we studied light and colour, temperature, heat and the measurement of heat. Apparently I was interested and worked well, and performed experiments with care and accuracy. Nevertheless, the report notes that here there were similar problems,

... She found the subject rather difficult at times, probably because she has never done any science before. She writes careful accounts of the experiments. Her explanations are often involved, possibly owing to her insufficient knowledge of English...

So much for the purely academic. The headmistress, in her Elocution report, correctly pinpoints a number of my stumbling-blocks. I am obviously having difficulties with the letters "r" and "th", as well as with some vowel sounds, and do not seem to have a very good ear. However, once again she comments on my enthusiasm and the pleasure I take in my work, and feels that these will help me to learn English. Interestingly, she claims that I am able "to make an intellectual approach to the subject", whatever that might mean, and that when given detailed inflexional markings for a set poem, I can recite it with the correct intonation. Curiously, the stage seems not to have presented any difficulties to me, for the report ends:

> Elisabeth was quick to learn her part in the play and to adopt appropriate actions, and I appreciated the way in which she helped the younger actors with their words and positions.

Obviously possessing a quick memory at this age, as well as having been a somewhat bossy older sister were standing me in good stead right now.

Physical exercises and singing are, of course, the subjects in which I am most backward. In singing lessons, I seem so shy and retiring that one is scarcely aware of my presence, and appear to have difficulty with pitch. However, I am so attentive and interested that I am obviously enjoying the songs, particularly English and Welsh folk songs whose simplicity appeals to me. Dalcroze Eurhythmics, as far as I can remember, involved appropriate and graceful movement to music. The report notes that though lacking physical poise and control, I show some rhythmic sense and that my earnest efforts have helped towards considerable improvement. Rhythmic sense, alas, is missing in Greek Dancing, for here I find rhythm difficult and produce jerky and stiff movements, and much the same is said about my performance in Physical Training, where I am particularly unrhythmical when coordination is required. However, both reports admit that thanks to my efforts, there is some progress, though clearly a great deal more was needed. In Games – Netball and Hockey, each of which require a separate report I do much better, and prove to be an enthusiastic player, with certain strengths and weaknesses which are all conscientiously noted.

Finally there is Arts and Crafts, in which I am making good progress, and respond well to suggestions. During the term I completed a leather pencil case, worked on the pottery wheel and finished two pots, designed a leather pochette as well as a felt tea cosy, and painted and varnished a wooden box. The instructor notes that I show some ability for design work, and that I managed cutting out and stitching well. The rest of the school year, as the next two reports mention, I seem to have far less time for Arts and Crafts, so obviously in my first term, I must have been encouraged to spend extra time somewhere where my lack of English did not matter, and where I could work without feeling constantly frustrated. This approach suggests that the school

possessed considerable flexibility and enjoyed wise guidance,
while the various reports show how conscientiously we were
supervised and taught.

After the Christmas holidays, we went back to school on 17
January 1940, enjoyed a brief break for the Easter weekend, and
then completed the Spring term on Tuesday, 9 April. Towards the
end of this term, the diary picks up again with an entry in English,
showing that by now I have mastered the language fairly well.
These two pages are dated "Eastersunday 1940", though the
coloured drawing at the top of the first page consists of pine-
branches, decorated with Christmas ornaments and a burning
candle. The second page, somewhat more appropriately, has three
rabbits hopping across the lawn, each carrying a basket of Easter
eggs. In fact, that Sunday afternoon, our large garden was the
setting for a traditional outdoor Easter egg hunt, an activity which
I had not encountered before coming to England. Though the eggs
were all of chocolate, in various sizes and coloured wrappings,
and searching for them in ingenious hiding places was exciting,
my diary ignores this event. The entry is far more concerned with
my religious obligations, as this passage shows:

> From now on I will write in German or English whatever I feel
> like, and keep you my dear book as a diary. The reason for this is
> that Brittain told us that is [sic] a good thing to keep a diary, and
> even if it comes at first a little bit difficult, one must make oneself
> write. Jean went away for the half holidays and as I had never
> been to the Catholic Church, [presumably, I meant alone] A. Evelyn
> would not let me go. So I had to [sic] with the rest to the Anglican
> Church. Oh, what agony of mind I have gone through before I
> could decide weather [the "a" is then crossed out] I ought to go or
> not. I seemed to have read in some Catechism that it is wrong to
> have the Holy Communion, but I had forgotten wether [sic] it also
> said anything about the service, and my concience [sic] told me
> that it was not wrong. So at last I went. Oh, how dissapointed
> [sic] I was. I always dislike pomp and there I could hardly bear it.
> Seb said she didn't like it either, but it was like a Catholic Church.
> At school we learn in James the first reign that the Puritans are
> very good people and so I was completely muddled.

This is the only English entry in the main part of the diary because
a few days later on Friday, 19 April, I switch back to my tidy
German script, explaining that I have had a letter from Fräuli, in
which she urged me to keep my diary as promised. Her reminder
has given me qualms of conscience, and therefore I decide to

write only in German, and to do so every day. Not surprisingly, this good resolution only lasts until 22 April, after which date the sporadic entries, though in German, are no longer written in script but use the Roman alphabet.

The two-page entry for the nineteenth goes on to describe the visit of Mrs. C.'s estranged husband to see his children. A slightly pompous but kindly man, he never forgot about me, and I still possess one of his gifts, a very large and beautifully illustrated copy of *Alice in Wonderland*. After tea, he made his goodbyes to Seb and to me, and then the C. girls accompanied their father outside. The diary notes that suddenly he turned back, came in again and gave me one shilling and sixpence, saying "for sweeties", pinched my cheek, and left before I could thank him properly. I am very embarrassed because I have never adequately expressed my gratitude for his various kindnesses nor given him anything in return, and have only been able to send him cards. I know that he is not well thought of in the C. household, and this makes me rather sad.

The next paragraph switches to my own family and shows that I am beginning to think in the language I now use every day. In the first sentence, when writing "I am waiting for letters", I make use of the preposition "für", obviously translating "for" from English, instead of using the correct German "auf". Various other mistakes are also beginning to creep in, but since it is not easy to find English equivalents, I will not attempt to translate them here. However, despite somewhat wobbly German grammar, the sentiments expressed in this entry sound genuine enough and suggest that I am fairly unhappy at the time of writing. One reason for this may be that we are between terms, and therefore are expected to be enjoying a brief holiday, but after the liberating experience of school, endless days at "Woodlands" where I always feel constrained and exposed to negative criticism, have become increasingly painful.

> At present I am waiting for letters, letters, letters. These are coming now very regularly from home, but I want more. News that I can leave soon, that they have found work, anything but this terrible waiting. I am also expecting a letter from Mrs. H. [George's foster mother], telling me that I may stay with her for a weekend.

The final paragraph notes that a new family has moved into the vicinity, thus providing me with another playmate. Our games soon attract a third girl with whom I have apparently played before, so she too appears to live in the neighbourhood. However, this unnamed girl and the newcomer now whisper so much together, that I feel left out and claim that playing with them gives me no pleasure, ending up exceedingly sorry for myself. As far as the diary is concerned, I seem to have enjoyed my paintbrush more than my pen, so that many of the pictures that head each diary page were done well ahead of time; even most of the blank pages that are left in the book already have such a decorated frieze at the top, sometimes executed with coloured pencils and sometimes with water colours. Consequently, these illustrations do not always fit the season or the text. However, for the entry on Saturday, 20 April, the bunny rabbits have all turned their back to the page, and this picture is most appropriate, given my mood that day.

> I came late for lunch because I had been out walking, but I didn't care... Marching along made me break out into the song "*Farewell, Thou my Beloved Homeland*", but when I reached the final verse, I burst into tears. Actually I had already been depressed all morning, because after breakfast Mrs. C. called me into her room to tell me that from now on I should start mending my own clothes, and that Mrs. H. couldn't take me for the weekend. The bedroom was filled with cigarette smoke and both windows were closed. And there I had to stay winding two balls of yarn instead of being able to play happily elsewhere, while she cheerfully read the paper. I brooded dark thoughts.
>
> And in the evening, when I wanted to go to bed early because I wanted to go to church the next day, she said: "I believe I told you that you could only go every other week because it is too early for Seb." Seb said that she would wake up in any case [which suggests that in her timid way, she was trying to support me] and I marched upstairs to bed.

Though I had already been told that I wouldn't be allowed to go to church the next day, I was obviously still hoping that Seb's intervention would somehow make my attendance possible, but of course it didn't and so, as the next entry shows, I was thoroughly miserable that Sunday.

> I woke up today when Seb started to get dressed – I couldn't go. I was so furious that I couldn't say a word at breakfast. Afterwards I went to the bathroom to wash my face with cold water. Otherwise I would have choked with anger. After that I picked a few flowers for Aunt Evelyn, so that she wouldn't think that I am sullen.
>
> I played all alone with the neighbour's child and asked her not to whisper with the other child when I was around. And she agreed.

The last entry in April simply says, "Since I have been lazy for so many days, now I will really start working." Just what that work entailed is not clear, but obviously Mrs. C. was quite justified in suggesting that I should start looking after my own things instead of leaving everything to Seb.

What made me so "lazy" over the holidays? No doubt the sense of having endless time stretching before me had something to do with my tendency to drift through the days. While the Spring term report praises the way in which I organise my time and draws attention to my industriousness, once away from school I seem to have lacked self-discipline as well as physical energy. Yet at school I was turning into an "able and effective player" at Netball and Hockey, becoming very good at tackling, and making considerable progress in the other physical disciplines as well. Academic subjects continued to be my forte, of course, with the beginnings of trigonometry in Mathematics, the Stuart period in History, and *Pride and Prejudice* as well as fairly advanced grammar in English. In Latin I was doing well, but rushing through some of the exercises rather too quickly and consequently carelessly, in a spirit of competition. It seems to me that I was competing with the other refugee girl, and that the two of us were ahead of the rest of the class. Seeing which one of us could outdo the other was really a game which we did not take very seriously, but the fact that we played it at all suggests that we were enjoying a new sense of security. While in Geography I was now producing very satisfactory maps – we were studying North America in general, and Canada in greater detail that term   drawing diagrams of apparatus in Science took me rather too long. Overall, Lois comments on the number of books I had read that term, on my general resourcefulness and progress along artistic and manual lines, and notes, "Elisabeth does not appear to have any one particular friend but enjoys the company of the whole group and takes an active share in the appearance of the group room. She is pleasant in her manner to all members of the community, responsive to suggestions and always ready for new experiences."

Numerous reports stress that I respond well to criticism, and benefit by showing marked improvement, which leaves one wondering why the criticism I received at home had such a negative effect on me. Undoubtedly it was not presented in a very helpful way, sometimes as unkind mockery, and frequently, as in most households, in the guise of scolding or nagging. Furthermore, every normal child shows greater readiness to accept constructive

criticism from outside the home. However there is also the fact
that the school allowed me more room to grow as an individual.
Every Garden School mistress calls me "Elisabeth" in her report,
while the C.s, with the best of intentions, wanted to integrate me
into English life as quickly as possible, and called me "Elizabeth".
That minor change of spelling seemed to deny yet one more facet
of my personal identity. Not being able to go to church was part
of the same problem. Force of circumstances made my weekly
attendance difficult, though this early in the war, it would not have
been impossible. Not only was I a naturally devout child; my religious
faith was also the one stable and abiding remnant of all that I had
had to leave behind when I crossed the Austrian border. The C.
family, with their strong humanism and their equally strong anti-
clerical bias, failed to take this into account, and did not recognise
how much misery all these enforced absences caused me.

Our Spring term ended on 9 April. Neither the school report
nor my diary seem to be very conscious of what was going on in
the world outside. After the first panic rush to evacuate children,
issue gas masks and institute drills, a time of nervous waiting
followed, known in Britain as "the Phoney War". This period
seemed to be drawing to its close when in April 1940, the Germans
successfully invaded Denmark and Norway. We returned to school
for the Summer term on 8 May. Two days later, the long waiting
came to an end with the German attack on France and the Low
countries. On 10 May 1940, the ineffectual Chamberlain was
finally forced to resign, and Winston Churchill assumed the
leadership of a country fighting for its life.

CHAPTER VII
THREAT OF INVASION

Towards the end of 1940, The Garden School finally published a brief account of the school activities that had taken place the previous Spring Term, and added a similar account for the Summer Term. Because of war shortages, these two accounts are extremely concise and are both contained in a one-page Bulletin, followed by "News of Old Girls". While the space devoted to the Spring Term contains no mention of the war, there are, not surprisingly, an increasing number of references to it in the Summer one. Under the heading "The School and the War", the Bulletin notes,

> We had two air raid alarms at the end of June. All members of the community were assembled quickly and in perfect order and quietness in the central corridor; the response was excellent. We whiled away the time with conversation, knitting and singing, and cocoa and biscuits before we returned to bed were much appreciated. We have now completed a good shelter, to the cost of which parents have contributed generously.

Under "Other Events" we learn that one music recital raised money for the local knitting fund, and another for the Red Cross, while the local Fire Brigade was able to hold an A.R.P. rehearsal in a building lent to them by the school. Sunday Service collections were sent to The Seamen's Mission and the Channel Islands Relief Fund. Many of the "Old Girls" were already involved in war work; one, a promising novelist who had joined the Air Transport Auxiliary, had been killed in a flying accident that July; several had gone to parts of the world which were becoming war zones – Copenhagen, now only reachable via the Red Cross, and Singapore and China, soon to be engulfed in even worse conditions.

If Seb had not forwarded a copy of this Bulletin to me in the U.S.A., I would never have known about all these events, even though I was still at the school when they were happening. No doubt boarders were more aware of such matters than day pupils, though we certainly attended the various music recitals – but then, music recitals were always being held for some good cause, so one hardly singled them out as being part of the war effort. Perhaps too, the school needed time to put everything into perspective, for despite all the facts belatedly chronicled in the Bulletin, with one exception, my school report for that Summer term contains no reference at all to wartime conditions. There were the usual comments about my making satisfactory progress in most subjects, and slowly improving even in those that demanded physical agility. Games, however, was the exception. In the previous terms I had done quite well at Field Hockey and Netball, sports which I thoroughly enjoyed, but in the summer, when we switched to Rounders, my report noted a number of problems. I suspect that not only did this particular sport demand a different type of coordination and muscular strength, but also, unlike Field Hockey and Netball, Rounders was not a very aggressive game, and thus gave me little chance to relieve frustrations. Nowhere in the Summer term report is there any mention of Cricket, though in memory I vividly recall this sport as one I was expected to play but did not understand in the least. I can still picture myself, somewhere in an outfield position, intensely bored, waiting endlessly for a ball which never seemed to come my way, so undoubtedly the boredom, which may have contributed to my doing rather badly, was real enough, even if it involved another game than the one I thought it had been. However, although my memory is somewhat faulty here, of one fact I am certain: whenever we played any sport which involved two competing teams, we called ourselves "Oxford" and "Cambridge". Without knowing anything about either university, I always opted for Oxford, a predilection that twelve years later would lead me there when at last I was able to return from the United States.

The one reference to the war which my school report for the Summer term contains can be found under Brittain's report for History. After stating that this term we completed the study of the Stuart period, including the Civil Wars, the Commonwealth and the Restoration, and assessing my work favourably, Brittain adds a new heading, that of "Civics". Under this title she writes as follows:

> It was made possible this term for everyone who wished to do so to listen once a day to the BBC news bulletins, but we continued to hold the weekly discussion group in order to provide opportunities for following the course of the War on the map, and for discussing and clarifying the events of the week in order to gain a fuller understanding of the trend of events. Elisabeth chose to attend these discussions.

This entry is extremely brief and factual. Is this only because Brittain has left herself little space on the page and did not want to start a new one? Or can the painful nature of the news which we were having to discuss account for this uncharacteristic brusqueness? Our Summer term ended on 23 July, amidst an unceasing list of disasters. Scarcely had we returned from our Spring break, when Hitler invaded Belgium and Holland. Despite fierce resistance, these were soon forced to surrender (and, as we were to learn much later, Tante Lily, my mother's socialist sister who had sought refuge in Brussels, disappeared from there without a trace when it fell on 17 May). Nine days later, the allied evacuation of Dunkirk had begun, and though we all cheered the little boats and pleasure crafts which braved German fire to rescue the men, completing their operation by 4 June, we were treating a major defeat as some kind of moral victory. Nevertheless, the country was bracing itself for invasion – by the end of May all signposts were ordered removed, in order to confuse advancing enemy troops as well as to uncover any spy who managed to land and would need to ask for directions from the local population. We were all so conscious of national security that even my diary occasionally omits place names and uses a dash instead! Soon the rest of Europe fell to the Nazis, for Italy entered the war on 10 June and decided to ally herself with the German side which appeared to be winning. On 14 June, German troops marched into Paris, and by the twenty-first, France had surrendered. All that seemed left to us was Churchill's magnificent and stirring rhetoric.

When the Germans occupied Guernsey without meeting any resistance on the last day of that June, it was hard not to expect them to land at any moment on the mainland. Churches were no longer allowed to ring their bells for normal services, since their tolling was now reserved for signalling the expected invasion. The countryside was full of wild rumours about enemy parachutists who were landing in such unlikely disguises as nuns' habits, which made Julia and me careful about whom we encountered when going back and forth to school, as well as watching out for what was going on overhead. Should we hear the ominous growl of a Junker or a Heinkel, instead of the reassuring sound made by a Spitfire – and indeed, we could tell the difference – we were expected to lie down flat on our tummies in the nearest ditch, covering our necks with clasped hands. The school instructed everyone how to put on their gasmasks, and we could never go anywhere without them. One slung the small, oblong box over one's shoulder like a handbag; in fact, if one could afford to replace the regulation case with a more expensive one, it did indeed look a little more like a handbag. While neither Julia nor I possessed a particularly elegant case, at least it was a step up from the standard issue and set us apart from the village. However, all children joined in singing a mocking little rhyme popular in the neighbourhood:

> Underneath the spreading chestnut tree
> Neville Chamberlain said to me,
> If you want a blinking gasmask free,
> You must join the A.R.P.

Occasionally we giggled over the self-importance various members of our Home Guard displayed, though really this was no laughing matter. Whatever other units elsewhere might have been like, when our local one drilled, one could see that it was singularly ill equipped to deal with the threat posed by tanks and heavy army equipment. Despite all this, Aunt Evelyn was not only sure that England would win in the long run, but did not really expect an invasion. However, in case the worst happened, she and Gillian were determined to rush at the enemy with pitchforks, while I planned on hiding in the nearest tree, and wondered what good that would really do. Needless to say, far away, my parents were frantic with worry about the safety of their children and doing what they could to get us across the U-boat infested Atlantic.

None of these events or circumstances appear in my diary, possibly because during the school year I was much too busy to write in it, especially since doing so in my native language was beginning to demand too much time and effort; and though I felt committed to these German entries, as long as the school was providing so much stimulation, I did not want to be distracted from my work in English. The latter was progressing well, helped by voracious reading, at this point chiefly the novels of Jane Austen. Nevertheless, the moment that our summer term ended the diary resumes, and from this point on contains daily entries until 29 September, which describes my arrival in New York. After that date there is only one more entry ten months later, this time written in English. By the summer of 1940, however, my German is already so poor, that an occasional sentence defies deciphering and I can only guess what I must have meant at the time. Many of the entries concern my difficulties with Julia, and only from late August on are there references to the war.

The entry for 23 July notes that "Today is the first day of the holidays" and states that I do not like holidays very much, especially when they are as long as these will be – two full months. The possibility of my leaving England soon must already have been in the air because I describe going to school to fetch something and saying goodbye to Toots. "She kissed me and I was considerably moved. I don't know if I'll ever see The Garden School again..." I lament, and then mention playing with the village children in the evening. The next morning I helped with the cooking, and in the afternoon I read and knitted. Apparently Aunt Evelyn drew attention to my assistance, perhaps in an effort to encourage me, but I always worried that such praise would make Julia jealous. The diary suppresses this reason and merely states, "I hate it when Mrs. C. puts a greater value on things than they really possess, for instance as regards my help in the kitchen about which she makes such a fuss." On the twenty-fifth, I am still homesick for school, for I write,

> Today I have a dreadful tummyache. I have decided not to trust anyone here too much. I am somewhat sad that I can't see Toots anymore, and without Brittain's help I can hardly bear it here. I find Seb's domesticity utterly repugnant and can only think how happy I would be with Brittain, for she understands me.

Poor dear Seb! Less than two years later I would be writing about her with deep admiration and affection, remembering her unobtrusive, ceaseless activity on behalf of the whole family, her hidden devotional life, as she read her Bible or prayerbook late at night when I was supposedly asleep, and her many kindnesses to me. Though she was far better educated than Fräuli and thoroughly enjoyed the novels which we read each evening, her approach to life was definitely a very practical one. My youthful intolerance fastened on Seb's concern with everyday household matters and dismissed her as someone who had little interest in heroic history or epic poetry. Doubtless her Calvinist upbringing could not entirely approve of that vivid imagination which won me so much approval at school, and we must have clashed on numerous occasions when I had my nose in a book instead of attending to crumpled clothing and loose buttons.

My stomach ache continued over the next day when – according to the diary – I did nothing at all, while on the following day, 27 July, the tranquillity of nature made me once again very unhappy and homesick. Also, I report reading a book which showed me what human beings are really like. Could I possibly be referring to Miss Austen's acute observations? The diary fails to elucidate this point but goes on to note,

... indeed, today I found them like that. After three months, Rowena returned today to us, along with Mrs. C. and Gillian who came back from London. She didn't pay the least attention to me and I felt hurt, even though she has a shallow nature. Suddenly I long for my old catechism. I still know the ten commandments, but can only remember the first, second, fifth and sixth of the fundamental truths. I have forgotten two. Also I use many swear words and am untidy. Mama will not be very pleased with me and I wish most earnestly that I had never needed to come to England.

Who else but Jane Austen would describe someone as possessing a "shallow nature"? And while my mother could sometimes be referred to by the childish appellation of "Mama", the Austrian equivalent of "Mummy", my brother and I usually called her "Mims". Hence the tone of this passage with its self-conscious concern that she might not be pleased with me suggests that here the more sophisticated "Mamá" is intended. Probably Miss Austen is also responsible for the fact that so many of the later diary entries refer to Aunt Evelyn as "Mrs. C.", particularly in her role as authority figure or when she does something which arouses anger or resentment which I dare not express openly. In the last few diary entries when I, about to be torn from the C. home, cling to her, she becomes once again "Aunt Evelyn". Lastly, what did I consider "swear words"? Even if older members of the C. family occasionally used mild expletives, surely Seb would not have allowed me to get away with anything like that!

According to the diary, on Sunday, 28 July, I didn't do anything, which presumably means that I did not help in the house or the garden, and did not go anywhere, since the entry states that I only read all day long and made dresses for my doll. The next morning I was much more active for I took my skipping-rope, hoping to become a little thinner. Today of course, such concern in a twelve-year old girl is quite usual, but it seems somewhat odd fifty years ago, especially since contemporary photos show that I really didn't need to worry about my weight. I also helped Mrs. C. with the spinach and read a little. The entry continues,

Mrs. C. took us swimming in the afternoon. J.[Julia] was very nice and that makes me uneasy. I suspect that the cat intends to pounce again. Anyhow, I must be on my guard. We went out in a rowboat and it was lovely. I found a water lily and wrapped it in a leaf. As we got out of the boat, J. threw the lily into the water. A.E. [Aunt Evelyn] made her fish it out again, and afterwards she said "sorry" to me. I have puzzled a great deal as to whether she did it on purpose or accidentally... In the morning I had a letter from

Mims [my mother], and I answered it in the afternoon. After Seb
had said "Good Night" to me, I continued secretly writing.

The next day I pretended to finish the letter to my mother, apparently
finished the night before, and then wrote to Onkel Martin to tell him
what works of Goethe I had been reading. Here is another puzzle.
Was I consciously trying to maintain my German, and where had
I found any volume of Goethe? The diary, of course, holds no
clues, though it contains occasional references to a library within
walking distance from which I used to borrow books. This could
only have been the little library in our nearest village, which is
most unlikely to have provided me with any German material,
though some of its holdings seem to have been surprisingly good.
My choices must have been reasonably mature ones, for the diary
records at least one instance when much to my annoyance, Julia
learned from Seb what book I had taken out and asked to borrow
it. On another occasion, Gillian seems to have helped herself to
my library book without bothering to tell me, so that eventually I
had to hunt for the book, and could not go to the library that day to
exchange it for another. The entry for the last day of July originally
contained only one sentence saying "Today absolutely nothing
happened." However, later on I seem to have remembered that
something *did* happen, because writing as small as I possibly
can, I have squeezed in two more sentences which say " Only my
'Report' came and I was quite pleased. Mrs. C. said nothing about
the school." Considering how much the comments of Brittain and
Toots mattered to me, it seems odd that I should not have noted this
as a red letter day at the time! Since I was quite pleased about the
report, I must have been allowed to read it or else Aunt Evelyn
told me what it contained. Perhaps she said nothing because she
felt that I had already received sufficient praise; given all the
wartime problems, she might also have been preoccupied by
weightier matters. If I felt hurt, or if I speculated as to the reason
for her silence, I had left myself no room for further comments.

Many of the diary entries begin or end with a comment on the
weather, a habit I had probably acquired in Austria where such
observations had been useful fillers for my summer journal. Thus,
for example, I note on 30 July that the morning was overcast and
there was a continuous light rain, while the first of August is
described as very hot, causing us once again to go swimming. I
also report making a new bed for a small doll that day, and though
I remember nothing about this venture nor what the doll looked

like, I can recall designing and sewing numerous clothes for her. Not that I had forgotten poor Trude, but given her size, neither the scraps of material at hand nor my limited skills were of much use. The next day, 2 August, the world of dolls receded into the background. The entry suggests that I have had the chance to talk to Rowena again and no longer consider her quite so shallow:

> Rowena left today for London, and later on Seb went too. Rowena and I talked about Brittain, and I am supposed to give her a "message" [this word is written in English presumably because I no longer know the German word] from Rowena. I stood for a long time, gazing after the bus which carried Seb to London, until it was completely out of sight. Then slowly I returned homeward, to a home which I really don't have....

Would Miss Austen have approved of so much ingratitude and self-dramatisation? Even worse was to follow the next day, 3 August, when I gave free rein to my imagination:

> Today Gillian went away for the whole day and Mrs. C., Julia and I went swimming at Marlow and afterwards had a picnic tea. Cake, chocolate and milk! I don't call that a picnic. What I wanted was bread and butter with cheese or sausage, and lemonade. We had a magnificent view – but it was only an *English* landscape! It seemed to me as if sometime in the future the river would run with blood, the fishermen would turn into wild soldiers and the peaceful folk taking a stroll would become a wild and fleeing peasantry...

Such lurid pictures seem to be a compound of wartime news, epic battles, scenes from Sir Walter Scott, and possibly some novel we were reading aloud over our evening knitting which was concerned with the French Revolution and involved the rescue of the little Dauphin. My lament that the landscape before me is only an English one suggests that once again I am feeling homesick, a supposition which is re-enforced by my references to quite different picnics long ago in Austria. Presumably I am also expecting the peaceful scene to be changed by a forthcoming invasion, but why is the tone so blood-thirsty and exultant? I suspect that unconsciously I am wanting to revenge myself against the two people with whom I am sharing this picnic since they are the ones who most often found fault with me. That I myself, more than anyone else, would be endangered by a German invasion does not seem to have entered my mind here.

The entry for 4 August notes that I played again with the village children and painted a little, which might well have involved decorating pages of the diary. On the other hand, I was also rather fond of painting Madonnas and Crucifixion scenes, unaware that from the window above Gillian could watch what I was doing in the courtyard. When she showed interest in my work, I was highly embarrassed because I did not want to display my religious feelings in any way. The entry, of course, does not mention what I was painting but turns to other matters. I am using my skipping-rope every day now. At teatime I am extremely clumsy with the breadknife and Mrs. C. is furious. Was I somewhat careless, or is that lack of coordination which the school had already noted to blame? If the latter, then getting angry with me only made matters worse. However, given all the worries with which she was faced, it is not too surprising that Aunt Evelyn would lose her temper with me occasionally; she probably controlled it more often than I realised. If my mother had exercised a little more restraint in Vienna, then my basic insecurity when faced with any authority figure would not have been so great and I would have been better able to cope with such criticism as came my way.

The next afternoon guests came for tea, and we all played deck tennis. Later on, Tammie, a neighbouring village child, and I made ourselves useful by collecting wood, but also engaged in a certain amount of boisterous play while doing so. "When she wanted to tickle me, and I, making a game of it, wanted to roll her over, she started crying," I note. Once again it was very hot and I mention spending some time writing, without specifying the subject, though I suspect that what I meant was creative writing. Unlike my painting, writing was a purely secular activity. Insofar as it involved my diary or letters to the family, it was done in German, but a novel which I started, and in which I naturally cast myself as the heroine, was certainly done in English. There were also a number of poems. All of this iuvenalia has been lost, except for a few lines addressed to Mary Tudor, which have survived in my history workbook:

> Mary at first had been
> At her reign's beginning
> A really po'plar Queen
> For her way was winning.

> Innocent young Lady Jane Grey
> Henry VII's great-granddaughter
> With her husband had to give way
> Followed by Mary's woe & slaughter.

This little rhyme is probably not typical of the kind of poetry which I was writing for my own pleasure but seems to have been an additional, though undoubtedly voluntary, piece of schoolwork in the Spring Term of 1940. More noteworthy for historical accuracy than for poetic skill, the lines are included in the section which shows the Protestant martyrs being burnt at the stake.

According to the diary, 6 August was again "boiling hot". I spent a good bit of it putting my things in order because Seb was coming home that evening. I also wrote to my parents and to other members of the family. At some point during the day, Mrs. C. took me with her,

> ... and I came to the heath from where, with only a few steps, one reaches my church. I hardly dared to look up. How can I describe my feelings when I found myself so close to my beloved church and yet could not enter it for at present I can no longer attend Mass – the Germans are responsible for that... We bought two ducks for Julia and she is supposed to pick them up tomorrow morning.

If 6 August upset me, the next two days proved even worse, the first owing to an encounter with Julia, and the second because of one with her mother. Julia and I were responsible for doing the dishes, and were supposed to take turns at washing and drying. 7 August I note that something peculiar happened today and go on to complain that for several days now, Julia has managed to do the washing up, leaving me with the unpopular drying. Apparently this particular day I succeeded in getting to the sink first, and when Julia objected, I pointed out to her that this was what had been settled:

> She said that was just temporary and anyhow, thank God, I had no authority in the house. I didn't answer her anything, and when she took a dishtowel, she pushed it right in my face. I didn't do anything, but continued calmly with the washing. Then she said "Please set down the plates the other way." I didn't say anything but did it, and when I forgot once, she said something. However, she must have worried that I would tell Mrs. C. for she let me wash, and afterwards she begged my pardon and told me that sometimes I made her very angry. Then she asked me if I would like to go with her ducks to the pond. I couldn't say "no", so I went, but it was horrible. I bled all over and ripped my dress, while she stood on the other side and wasn't hurt a bit.

Poor Julia! I don't know how much the separation of her parents had affected her, and I doubt that anyone knew, since she was extremely introverted. Quite apart from her natural jealousy of me, she was also finding adolescence particularly painful. Tucked into my diary are a few pages, scribbled in pencil on my thirteenth and on my fourteenth birthday, in which I pour out how miserable I feel, not knowing who I am, how horrible I am to everyone around, and how I hate all the world, and myself most of all. While these pages do not belong to the present account, rereading them now helps me to understand better why Julia behaved as she did. At the time, since I myself was still an exceedingly naïve child, I could not make head or tail of her moods.

Like Julia, I was regularly given pocket money, which Aunt Evelyn remembered better than my father. Needless to say, if ever she forgot, normally I did not remind her, though towards the end of my stay in England, I had to ask for my pocket money because I was using it to buy presents for everyone, not only for my parents but also for those I was leaving behind. My involvement with this task led to an unpleasant confrontation with Aunt Evelyn, as the diary reports for Thursday, 8 August. That day I had bought embroidery silk and had started right away to work on some mats for my mother. Apparently I was following a new pattern because the required stitch caused me some trouble since I had never attempted it before. While I thus engaged, a friend of Mrs. C.'s stopped by briefly on her bicycle. Naturally, Mrs. C. came out to greet her, but as soon as I saw Mrs C., I rushed over to show off my embroidery: The diary entry, which accepts such behaviour as natural, goes on to show that even Seb sometimes lost patience with my self-absorption.

> Seb said, "Be quiet. One doesn't talk about one's own concerns when one receives guests." Later, Mrs. C. called me in and held me a long lecture. She looked at my embroidery and said that it was horrible and that I would have to start all over. Then she asked me why I had left dead flowers on the lawn, called me a little monster, and was really beastly to me. I went out and cried in the woods and was sorry that I had picked blackberries for her.

The next day Mrs. C. left for London, and I was probably considerably relieved, although the diary merely notes her departure without any comment.

A number of diary entries show how often I think about my grandparents. After having worked all day on my embroidery on 11 August, for instance, in the evening I have to do gardening and afterwards feel so chilled that Seb takes me for a walk to warm up again. We go past a garden, where I see an elderly lady whom I have encountered before in the library. I note that her husband kindly gives me two plums, while she resembles my grandmother. The next day a stranger reminds me of my grandfather. But that entry – for 12 August – is worth quoting in full:

Today a gentleman came for tea. He was a poet and Jewish, and he had funny, crinkly hair on his head. His conversation was very intelligent, and I wished that I could have been grown-up because then I could have talked with him. In the morning when I went to the village to get my embroidery silk, I had to wait two-and-a-half hours for the shop to open. Because I walked up and down, a little golden-haired boy ran after me. In the evening, as I walked through the other village, I saw a man who bore such an uncanny resemblance to Opapa [my grandfather], that I felt really insulted when I saw him chatting with the landlady of a common inn.

The following day I received the first letter my parents wrote after leaving New York and settling temporarily in Buffalo. I was so excited that I showed the letter to Mrs. C., unfortunately overlooking the fact that my parents were responding to some derogatory remarks I had made about Seb. Today, of course, I can no longer recall what had bothered me, while the diary entry only notes cryptically, "It was something about the 'At Home'", with the words "At Home" being written in English. Naturally Seb asked me about the letter, and I had to invent some quick excuse. Mrs. C. went to London again on 16 August, and this time there is the comment, "I don't mind that she goes but I wish that she would take J. with her." However, since Mrs. C. only stayed away one night, I would not have had much respite. The day she came back, Gillian went with her father and aunt to Windsor, leading me to comment "Nobody cares very much for the family", apparently once again referring to Mrs. C.'s estranged husband. As on many other occasions, I tagged along with Seb who had some errands to attend to. We visited a house in a very beautiful large garden, filled with fruit trees, and I was given a few plums, but was either hungry or else very greedy, since I longingly gazed at some others I particularly wanted. The whole brief entry concludes with a sentence, clearly added on later, noting that I went to the library and got out a book which looked nice. These looks, however, proved deceiving for already the next day there is a note in brackets "*Wiudyhaw* was a terribly vulgar book." Unfortunately, today it would be difficult to disentangle the obviously garbled title, but even if one could do so and discover what book this was, there is no way of establishing on what grounds I condemned it.

    Except for this postscript regarding my unfortunate literary choice, the rest of the long entry for 18 August is entirely devoted

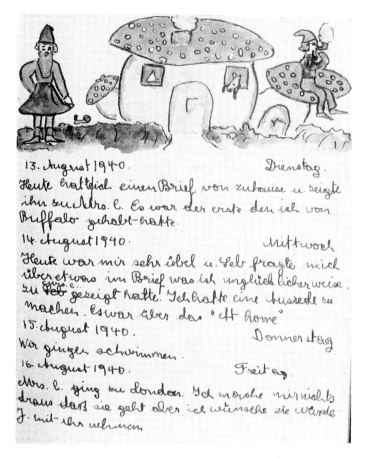

Although this illustration shows the influence of Germanic folktales, as far as the writing is concerned, I am no longer able to express myself in idiomatic German.

to describing a picnic by the Thames, which clearly shows the kind of problems I encountered with Julia:

"You must keep holy the Lord's day!" Let's see how holy I kept it! I had worse fights than ever before, and I was very unhappy. We went in the car to have a picnic by the river. Julia intended to take her two ducks and said that I could have her two little ships. So I got Trude [my big doll] ready and the two ships. When Julia saw them she said, "You can certainly have them, but take care of them." I said "yes" but didn't take them after all. Anyhow, I helped her with her ducks, but in the end she didn't take them along either. Later on, as she sat in a tree and I was fooling around at the water's edge, she said "How I'd like to throw you in!" and I answered,

"I'm sure you would, but I won't give you the opportunity." I forgot my flowers. In the car [presumably as we were getting in, preparing to go home, since Mrs. C. did not see it], suddenly without any reason, she punched me on the nose. After a while she said, "I am sorry. Does it hurt?" I said, "yes" and turned away. For days now, she has been doing all the washing again. Today, halfway through, she asked if I wanted to do it, but I said "no, thank you". After some time she asked me if I would go on feeling angry and offended forever. I said that I didn't know and that I couldn't look into the future, even though I know very well that I will *never* forgive her. However, she was satisfied with my answer because she laughed and asked me, "Do you know what you are talking about?" And I said, "no?"

Tormented herself, Julia could not help tormenting me. Perhaps the relationship between two siblings of the same sex, especially if one of them is a fosterling, is always more tense than that between brother and sister because a different kind of rivalry is involved. Although George and I sometimes quarrelled, we did so without any element of viciousness and/or bullying on either side; for though I was bossy, there is a vast difference between bullying and bossiness. Now, even when we were apart, I continued to feel responsible for my brother, and missed him very much. The greater geographical proximity, on which Mrs. C. had insisted, did not really help us to get together, and though I vaguely remember one car ride to visit George after he was moved to the farm in Hants, even that meeting may not really have occurred, and what I am recalling is merely the journey to take him to his new home. My brother's foster family were kindly, unpretentious folk, as attuned to social concerns as Aunt Evelyn was, but without her intense interest in literature and the arts. Given wartime conditions, less than ever could I expect that she would want to drive me down to Hants. However, my brother and I wrote to one another fairly frequently, and on 20 August I note that I had a letter from George, thanking me for the sailboat which I must have sent him for his birthday on the sixteenth. The letter seems to have been longer than usual and I was very glad to get it. The following day my parents wrote again very cheerfully:

> ... full of hope that I would soon be able to come. For that is what they think after receiving the letter which I wrote them from the Consulate. It started me thinking....

There still exists an impressive foolscap "Certificate of Identity" issued by the Home Office in lieu of a passport on 3 August 1940, bearing my smiling picture, complete with National Health glasses, on its first page. The scrap of paper containing my signature which is pasted underneath this photo suggests that, given my age, no personal attendance was necessary, and that Aunt Evelyn handled all the paper work for me. The reverse side, stamped by the American Consulate in London, granting me an Immigration Visa, is dated 26 August 1940. Furthermore, a postcard despatched from the "Refugee Children's Movement, Ltd." at Bloomsbury House, 26 August 1940, confirms: "We have obtained your American Visa today, so there will be no need for you to come to the Consulate again." Obviously then, on at least one occasion, U.S. officialdom had required a personal interview, and while at the Consulate that day, I had apparently written to my parents. The diary, however, which faithfully records the daily activities of the entire summer, appears to leave no room for such a visit! Also, why is the last sentence left incomplete? What are the thoughts that I do not wish to put on paper? Getting away from Julia was one thing; but, though the diary does not say so at this point, my final destination was quite another. Perhaps now that this vague hope seemed to be becoming reality, I may have been allowing reactions to surface which the diary does not want to acknowledge, but which I remember distinctly.

Meanwhile, on the surface, life at "Woodlands" went on much as usual. On 22 August, two of Mrs. C.'s friends came to visit and we played charades. Priggish, and with little sense of humour, my diary indignantly considers such frivolous portrayals an affront to the heroes and great personages being represented in this game, but notes that I didn't say anything about my feelings. The entry for the next day is the first one which deals directly with wartime circumstances since I mention seeing car loads of soldiers going somewhere and then coming back again. On their return journey, a few of them waved to me, but I felt that if they knew that I wasn't English, then they wouldn't have waved. That same day, for once, Julia tried to be nice and offered to help me with the green beans, which must have meant that I had to get them ready for cooking; however, I didn't find her assistance very useful, since I comment that it did more harm than good. The next day, Saturday the 24 August, I completed the mats that I was making for my mother and put them on the table, to see what they would look like. Perhaps I also wanted someone else to see them and praise me, but this does not seem to have happened. Mrs. C. returned from a day or two in London and although I had begged her not to do so – fear of Julia again? – she brought me back a little chocolate. She also brought with her the family friend who had conducted the ballet classes I had attended in London the previous year. I was somewhat surprised that Antonia kissed me the same way as she kissed everyone else and note that I was a little disappointed by her, though the diary does not explain why, and only notes that I had forgotten what she was like and needed to get used to her again.

The house in London and all her other fiscal affairs were not the only reason for Mrs. C.'s brief and frequent journeys that August, since she was also devoting considerable effort to making travel arrangements for myself and for my brother. Besides the need to obtain U.S. visas and scarce space on some passenger ship, there was the further problem as to who would pay our fare. Mrs. C. generously arranged to look after me, paying the price of my ticket in instalments, but neither she nor my brother's foster family could manage further outlays. My father was still preparing to retake his medical exams so as to be allowed to practise in his new domicile. Hence my parents had absolutely no money at all, and for the time being depended on whatever menial jobs my mother could pick up as well as on the help of various committees. Many other refugee children must have faced a similar dilemma. Eventually the Catholic Committee for Refugees, which originally had been prepared to sponsor our education, came to the rescue and guaranteed a loan to my parents. The Quakers, to whom we owed our initial escape from Austria, now collected those youngsters who were able to leave England and made all necessary arrangements for our journey, but with so many children at risk on one side of the Atlantic, and desperate parents on the other, it was impossible to process all of them as fast as the critical war situation seemed to demand. Mrs. C. pleaded, cajoled and pulled strings to get my brother and me safely away as soon as possible. Though I was aware of some of these difficulties, I did not grasp their full extent, and so could not really appreciate all the efforts that she was making on my behalf. The fact that Julia had resolutely refused to leave England, although overseas relations had offered to take her, made me feel even more ambiguous about my forthcoming journey.

CHAPTER VIII
BETWEEN HERE AND THERE

While consulates and committees were considering my fate, I myself was torn between my old heroic code and the principles I was unconsciously absorbing from Jane Austen's romantic novels, with their strong moral bias and realistic outlook on life. On the one hand was the example of the Greek warriors who had never fled from battle; the sorer the need, the less likely had they been to save themselves by running away. Since England had offered me shelter when I was in the greatest distress, how could I desert this country now, and behave like a rat leaving a sinking ship? Was I not exhibiting the utmost ingratitude as well as shameful cowardice? Jane Austen, on the other hand, reserved her severest censure for any selfish and inconsiderate behaviour which made others suffer. Looked at objectively, in what way could I really help the English war effort? Was I not simply one more mouth to feed, at a time when there was increasingly less to go around? Had I any right to put further burdens on this country? If arrangements were made for me to go, then go I must.

If the idea of leaving was difficult to face, the thought of where I was going made matters worse. Aunt Evelyn, like many others of her class and generation, believed that the U.S. had behaved badly in the First World War, allowing Britain to exhaust herself fighting Germany all alone for almost three years, before stepping in at the last minute. Now in the Second World War, the pattern seemed about to be repeated. Britain's considerable economic decline after 1918 was largely blamed on what was perceived as lack of American support when most needed; more disasters were expected this time round, though as yet no one could foresee the end of the British Empire. The resultant moral indignation was coupled with resentment – never expressed but clearly lying below the surface – that this upstart nation of colonial bumpkins could behave like that and get way with it! Nevertheless, despite these feelings, everyone counted on U.S. supplies and on whatever help would come from across the Atlantic. In particular, we worried how far Congress, urged on by President Roosevelt, would help our war effort, and therefore listened faithfully to the weekly radio transmissions from America to Britain. However we were not averse to biting the hand that fed us. Thus, the only reason why I remember that the broadcaster was called Raymond Gram Swing is that at whatever point – either at the beginning or at the end of his talk – he started to give his name, all of us, led by our elders, would chant it in unison with him, mockingly exaggerating his accent and intonation. Given these circumstances, I could hardly be expected to have a very high opinion of this country to which I was going to be sent. The famous Edward R. Morrow had not yet won the admiration of the whole British nation, nor did I know that Henry James, an American, was one of Aunt Evelyn's favourite authors. Instead, all around me I heard frequent ridicule directed at gum-chewing "Yanks", at America's total lack of culture and at U.S. nomenclature, exemplified by their absurd emphasis on middle names or initials as well as by their propensity to appoint public figures whose ludicrous, polysyllabic names sounded Germanic rather then English. While some of these critical remarks might have gone over my head, I registered enough of them to realise that, in Nancy Mitford's terminology, America was definitely non-U. Not surprisingly, I too accepted this world view; the resultant snobbery made me hate the idea of having to leave civilised England to go and live in such an undesirable, barbarian country.

None of these sentiments are recorded in my diary, although by the end of August the question of my departure seemed to be so close to resolution, that such feelings must have been in the forefront of my consciousness. However, by this time the diary no longer plays the role of a true journal to which I can entrust "all the secret joy and sorrow in the depths of my heart" as that first entry in January 1939 naïvely claimed I would do. Rather, the book has become a chronicle which only describes emotional responses when these flow directly from some event that is being reported, and even then, tends to censor them, leaving the lost poems that I composed at the time as the only real outlet for some of my inmost thoughts. The reticence which these later diary entries display is not caused by fear of prying eyes, for after all, I was writing in a foreign language, and furthermore the diary was kept locked at all times. Rather, my reluctance to express certain matters was based on a sense of what was and was not fit for such a means of communication. There is even one occasion, when I refuse to put down a detailed account of what actually happened; thus, the entry for Sunday, 25 August reads:

> Today I went into the woods. Although I love you, dear book, and
> trust you, nevertheless I can't tell you about my druid-like actions.
> They are too sacred.– I lost the key of my book.

Undoubtedly it is significant that the day was Sunday and that, owing to wartime conditions, I was now totally unable to go to church. Deprived of Mass, Sunday mornings seemed strangely empty and hence, filled with an overwhelming need for ritual and worship, on the spur of the moment I invented my own. As far as I can remember, while walking in the wood which one could enter by crossing the road from our house, I found a small clearing penetrated by sunlight. This inspired me to place carefully chosen flowers on a large, moss-covered stone there, as a sacrifice to the presiding deity of the place; just who that might be I wasn't quite sure, but my reference to "druid-like actions" suggests a kind of nature worship. I approached the stone as if in a procession; perhaps I even tried to perform some kind of symbolic dance, vaguely based on movements learnt at The Garden School. Then, bowing reverently and backing out, I left the clearing. Long ago, my experimental worship of Zeus had been cut short by fear and guilt; this time, no such feelings marred my "sacred" actions. Nevertheless, though the little wood was extremely close to the C. cottage, I never returned to repeat this ritual.

The entry for the next day begins with rejoicing that I have found the key for my diary again. It goes on to note that our weekend guest was returning to London, and that,

> ... the others almost cried when we talked about the fact that London had been bombed and that there had been a big fire there. [This must have taken place 24 August when the first German attack on London occurred.] I could not cry. Didn't I cry enough already when I heard on 17 August that Vienna and Frankfurt had been bombed? And J. had to console me. I felt so miserable that I even let a *caterpillar* live. [We liked to kill these pests, which were destroying our fruit and vegetables, and usually got great satisfaction from squashing them.]

Surprisingly, it was Julia who apparently found me in tears when the cities I knew and loved were being bombed, and tried to comfort me. Nevertheless, the rest of that entry concerns another run-in with her, for in the afternoon, when we are both picking fruit, she wants to make sure that I don't take any from *her* tree. The next day, 27 August, brought more squabbles. The clothes which Julia had outgrown were being passed down to me, a fact which she resented. In someone going on fourteen, this is hardly surprising since what we wear tends to become part of ourselves; to be confronted daily by these outer shells of oneself, now hanging on a clumsy usurper, must be galling for any confused adolescent who has difficulty coming to terms with her own body. If Julia was troubled by such sentiments, then I can sympathize with her today. At the time I felt so degraded and indignant that, without deliberately planning to do so, I threw pebbles after her. Either my aim was poor or the stones were very small because the diary entry mentions the episode without following it up:

Today we went swimming. We went to fetch J's coat which now belongs to me. J. very unkind about it. Without really knowing what I am doing in the water, whenever I fetch up a stone from the bottom, I throw it towards her. I swim twenty-four widths. I misunderstood her friendliness [no explanation as to when this had been displayed] since she is absolutely beastly when we wash up after tea. As usual, she does the washing and I go to bed very early.

This particular situation is only partially resolved the following day, 28 August:

I tell Seb that I won't accept anything any more from Julia. She tells Mrs. C. about it. Result: She [J. presumably] is very gracious. She tells me that she will go swimming with me. On the way she says that she didn't think that I would take her remarks about the coat so to heart. I am weak-minded and say, it is all right, and usually I do not take anything to heart very long. Although I wanted to say, it isn't a good thing always to go around saying "I am sorry", and then to do it all again. In the afternoon, J. teaches me how to ride a bicycle, although it is difficult for her not to become impatient with me. I go for a walk with Seb and take both dolls. We speak about the U.S.A. I fall down and scrape my knees. Consequently I decide to make a carrier for Trude, and once again abandon the socks [which presumably I was knitting.] In the morning I hear that at long last I have received a visa.

The diary entry for the next day is brief and ambiguous owing to a misleading preposition. "I can't help showing my fear towards Julia", I write, but whether I mean that I am afraid of Julia and of what she will do if she loses patience with me, or that I am afraid of bicycling and let Julia know this, isn't clear. In any case, the second sentence completes the entry: "No bicycle lesson".

By now we were getting frequent reports of bombing. Some histories of the Second World War claim that "The Battle of Britain" embraces the period between July to September 1940, since Germany started its bombing raids in mid-July. However, the heavy bombing, particularly of London, did not begin until August, and many accounts consider 30 August the starting date of this brief but crucial campaign over the skies of England.

Ultimately, by mid-September, when the Luftwaffe had lost far more planes than the R.A.F., Hitler was forced to postpone his plans to invade Britain, and never again got another chance. Unaware of the momentous events being set in motion, my diary entry for 30 August mentions only that Mrs. C. has gone to London, though I do not seem to realise how dangerous this might be. A letter from home has come, presumably from my parents to Mrs. C., and I feel sure that it is the answer to whether or not I should go. (Presumably Aunt Evelyn had suggested a careful weighing of the alternatives, pointing out how dangerous such a journey across the U-boat infested Atlantic would be for a child). I go blackberry-picking with Gillian. Then follows the terse comment, "More bombs".

The last day of August, my departure for the U.S. is ratified and my diary is proof of my mixed reactions. The entry notes,

> ... I hear that my leaving is confirmed. Very glad. Money has been found for George's ticket. J. is at first horrible, but then *very* nice. She tells Seb that she intends going to —. I wonder if that means that she wants to give me a bicycle riding lesson. I go with Seb. Afterwards J. seems sorry that I have to go to bed. I cry for a long time because I don't want to leave England. Gillian hears me.

The curt "very glad" in response to the news that my journey to the U.S. is confirmed may indicate unwillingness to give way to emotions, though on the other hand I felt no need to conceal tears over having to leave England. Of course being simultaneously glad and sorry is quite possible to our complicated human psyche, even if this sounds like the logic of *Through The Looking Glass*. Considering that I had repeated conversations with Seb about America, I was at least interested in the subject. However it is equally possible that I wasn't very glad at all but felt that it was only proper to respond with some sign of pleasure. Certainly, the copious tears that were to accompany my departure from England cannot compare with those few I had earlier shed for Austria, nor was my occasional homesickness for family and native land ever as intense as the longing with which I was to remember my English home.

Whatever my true feelings at the end of August, for the next two weeks life at "Woodlands" continued as normally as wartime conditions permitted. There are the usual squabbles with Julia. On 1 September she appears to have been very impatient – the diary does not report why – and throws a bread crust at me. Later on a "horrible looking" woman comes, probably to see Mrs. C., and when I imitate her, Julia "gives me one of her looks", although

I know that she too hates that woman. I write home and work a
little on my Latin. The entry continues,

> ... I write my book [i.e. the novel which I was composing]. Present
> Julia and me symbolically, but so changed that it isn't obvious.
> We have a pleasant wintery supper [presumably, when it was
> already growing dark] without Gillian or Julia. We talk about
> Switzerland and everyone is a little depressed. I think about Tyrol,
> Carinthia and Velden.

The next day we go for another picnic and Julia behaves so
miserably towards me that I conclude by saying "I now hate
picnics". Actually, here as elsewhere, I label Julia's conduct as
"impolite", undoubtedly because by now my German vocabulary
is so faulty that it possesses no other adjective to describe her
behaviour towards me. Aware of this inadequacy, the diary adds
"etc." to indicate a situation which is beyond my power to express
in German. However, for the moment at least, part of my mind
seems to be turning towards the forthcoming journey because I
comment that when we went swimming and I crossed the bridge,
on looking into the water below, I felt as if I were on a ship.

On 3 September, I report walking with Seb and talking about
America again. Of far more import than such a remote subject,
however, is the fact that Julia has got herself a permanent wave,
and that I have been out picking blackberries for Mrs. C. The
juxtaposition of these two facts strikes me as suspiciously priggish
and self-righteous, as if I considered that Julia was being silly
and vain, while I showed proper consideration. Certainly Julia
agonised endlessly over her hair, and never got any sympathy
from me, especially not on this occasion, when she sneaked off to
the village salon without first obtaining approval for taking such
a drastic step. Only in one way were we both alike – neither of us
liked getting up in the morning and Seb frequently got cross
because she had to call us so often. In fact, a big falling-out
between Seb and me occurs on 4 September, which I claim is
primarily her fault, though the diary shows that most of it must be
blamed on my laziness in the morning, and contrariness at night:

> Seb wouldn't talk to me today, and it's all due to her own silly
> stubbornness. This morning, after she had called me repeatedly to
> get out of bed, I asked her to do up my buttons, to which she
> answered, "No, I won't. I am going downstairs for breakfast."
> Thereupon I answered something or other a bit impertinent. The
> same thing, or something similar, happened in Julia's room. So
> Seb told Gillian who fetched us for breakfast and gave us a good

scolding. Although Seb had threatened to do so, she didn't tell Mrs. C. I had been hoping a little that she would [why??]. In the evening both of us [i.e. Seb and I] were ready to make up again, but when she turned off the light, foolishly, she took my book away from the table and so I turned my back on her. Whereupon, very offended, she left the room without saying Good Night. I called after her, but she didn't come. I felt a *little* contrite but it was largely her fault.

However, I seem to have learnt my lesson. The next morning, I got up as soon as I was called, and note that "Without saying anything, we are friends again". Later that day Julia and I went swimming and for once got along very well. Although I carefully put a dash instead of a place name, our destination must have been High Wycombe, because the diary goes on to mention my desire to buy cork mats, which I can remember obtaining at the local Woolworth's. This shop which offered serviceable and attractive household goods for as little as sixpence, must have been a gold mine for many a child with limited funds seeking suitable Christmas and birthday gifts. By now I was busily gathering together all the presents I wanted to leave behind or take with me, and therefore whatever I didn't make myself, I bought there. However, under those circumstances I needed my pocket money, and Aunt Evelyn thought that she had already given it to me the week before. The diary entry notes that I had to ask Mrs. C. for it and that she did not want to believe me. She obviously had no idea how hard I found it to ask for money.

The following day, 6 September, was one filled with fear. Not only were there bombs, but Seb also had to go up to London, probably to clarify her status as an alien. Although we had our disagreements, I always felt more lonely and exposed when she wasn't there. This explains why I appear to have been so lost, gazing after the bus that had carried her to London on 2 August, and why on this later occasion I displayed such possessiveness in my encounter with Julia. The diary entry describes the day as follows:

I must recall now what happened in the night. Around three o'clock or thereabouts suddenly I heard an enormous noise. It was a bomb, very nearby. I could hear the German aeroplane, but no British plane. I was a little afraid. Mrs. C. and Seb discussed for a long time whether or not we should go downstairs. They decided that we shouldn't, and I chatted with Seb until four when I went back to sleep. This morning, Seb went to London. When I saw that Julia was carrying her suitcase, I said "*I* will go." She looked at me and then said, "Then go ahead." I accompanied Seb to the bus, and was somewhat afraid coming back, but nothing happened. This evening I wanted to go for a walk so that I could compose some poems. Mrs. C. also wanted to go somewhere, and J. with her. So J. said to me "What are you going to do?" and I replied quite sharply, "I want to go out." But Mrs. C. said that all of us should go together, and I had to go with them. At one point J. turned around and smiled at me, and I smiled back. On the way home I started feeling sick, and I knew that I was afraid of bombs or of something that I didn't know. Mrs. C. asked me if I would prefer not having to sleep alone, but I said that it was alright and that I wasn't afraid. When I was in bed, I tried to figure out what my feelings were, but couldn't do so because my brain was in such a whirl.

Hans caught a mole and we had to pull him away from the poor thing.

Bombs and fear of the unknown, and in the midst of it all, the most ordinary of occurrences. Good old Hans always came along on our walks across the common and through meadows, fields and woods, using such outings to rush ahead and start a dig, apparently looking for moles. Yet until I saw this diary entry, I did not remember that he had ever actually caught one. In fact, far more memorable – though not in the diary – is the occasion when we came upon him just as he discovered that there was a live mole confronting him in the hole which he had been digging out. Startled by this unusual event, Hans hastily beat a retreat, but the next moment he recovered, and ignoring our laughter, bounded away in the opposite direction, and busily started digging another hole there.

Although Seb is still away on Saturday, 7 September, there is no further reference to my being afraid. "Nothing special happened all morning", says the diary, but over lunch, they (presumably Gillian, Julia and their mother) had a row, and consequently we didn't go blackberry picking. Once again, the entry is largely concerned with Julia:

.... Instead, Julia and I went swimming at —. Afterwards we had a picnic with chocolate, and I went over a narrow bridge, at first very, very slowly like a snail, but later much quicker. Suddenly I got the idea to sit down in the middle of the bridge and start writing. J. splashed me with water, at first for a minute seriously, but then in fun.

We had supper and then listened to Beethoven's Fifth Symphony. J. asked me afterwards if I wanted to wash up, but I said, "No thank-you and I hope that you don't mind". She said, "No, not at all". So from now on I can only blame myself if I don't get the chance to wash up. She was nice the whole evening, and I

helped her to pick up the broken bits of a water glass. The bombs
have damaged a great deal in London.

By now the so-called "Blitz terror" had started, but it does not
appear to be uppermost in my mind since it takes broken bits of
glass to remind me of London under siege. Had I forgotten that
Seb was there, and didn't I worry about her at all? Or was I
keeping a stiff upper lip?

The next day, Sunday, the air attacks came closer to us. Given
the grave military situation, the Government had designated it as
a special day of prayer, and I felt that attendance at some church
or other was my patriotic duty.

> Friday morning I had asked Mrs. C. if I could go to the chapel,
> and since she had thought that it wouldn't be safe, naturally it was
> totally out of the question today. Therefore, since it was a National
> Day of Prayer, I went along with the others. This time we did not
> go to the village but to —. The sermon and the prayers were *very*
> good, the whole church was filled, and I liked it very much...
>
> In the afternoon I wrote home and gathered acorns for Gillian.
> In the evening, when we heard the warning sirens and I put on my
> dressing gown, Julia came into my room with tears in her eyes
> and said, "Elisabeth, I am sorry that I have been so beastly to you
> all these last days" and she kissed me. I could truthfully say that
> these last days she had been very nice to me. We had a jolly time
> downstairs [from now on, until the all-clear sounded, we always
> gathered in the living-room on the main floor]. The bombing of
> London continues and many people have lost their homes.

Owing to the excitement of the previous night and concern about
the bombs falling on London, the following day, Monday 9
September, I did not feel at all well, but did not tell anyone about
it. The diary entry notes,

> This morning I felt terribly sick, However, since I didn't want to
> seem ungrateful to J., I went with her to gather acorns. She was
> very nice to me. In the afternoon, however, I got a considerable
> number of her "looks" again. In the evening, all of us went for a
> walk, and I am ashamed to admit that at night I cried a little in bed
> because I felt so sick. In my imagination I died a number of times
> before I dropped off to sleep. Finally it started drizzling and it was
> freezing cold.

Luckily by the next morning I had recovered and was feeling
well enough to try to hold my own against Julia and to get ready
for Seb's return, though I worried whether or not she would be
able to get back, given all the London raids.

I woke up feeling quite well and cheerful but I think that I have a little bit of a cold. The weather is somewhat better [the comparative form of this adverb sounds much the same in English as in German, and quite unconsciously I have used the English form]. J. much as usual. In the morning she is angry because I ask for brown toast which she also wants. She says that I always do whatever she does and calls me —. [Probably the word was "copy-cat" and I couldn't translate it.] That's absolute nonsense because I didn't know what she was having, and I say so. After all, I can eat what I want, but I don't tell her that. I clean my room thoroughly because Seb is coming back this evening. I wonder if she'll be able to come.

At lunch time there's another row, and naturally I take no part in it. J. doesn't want to hold my plate [presumably when it had to be passed forward to have food put on it], and Mrs. C. has to tell her to do it. I can't understand how she can behave like that after having been so nice the last few days... Seb comes back and brings me darning wool and eau de cologne.

On the whole, I got along better with Gillian than with Julia. Much more of an extrovert than her younger sister, and extremely pretty, with dark, curly hair, Gillian seemed unconcerned about her appearance and could be a bit of a tom boy. Despite her tendency to anaemia – she had to drink special tonic wine with her lunch every day – she gave the impression of being a vivacious and robust girl. While already helping on the land, she still found time to paint and particularly enjoyed depicting the surrounding landscape, occasionally leaving an unfinished canvas stashed away in a convenient hedge or hayrick. My diary for 11 September notes that I accompanied her to collect some such picture, but that we could not find it and presumed that it had been stolen. On our way through the village we met people from London whose house lay in ruins. 11 September was the day when both Buckingham Palace and St. Paul's were damaged in the raids, though the news was slow to reach us. Most of my diary entry is concerned with an afternoon picnic at which we played silly games with some adult friends and how foolish I found the whole business. As usual, I kept this opinion to myself. "J. not very nice but bearable" the entry concludes.

Although it rained quite a bit the next day, a moment later the sun would come out again. I commented that the weather seemed more like April than like September, and delighted in a beautiful rainbow. After I had finished knitting my socks, "I went for a walk in the meadows and philosophised", whatever that might mean. The socks must have been intended as a present which I was secretly making, because the following morning, I had another row with Seb over the state of my clothes, whereupon she told someone who wasn't supposed to know that my socks were finished, and I felt very annoyed. More important than all that, however, is the fact that once again, Aunt Evelyn was in London, and by now I was sufficiently alert to the danger this involved to note that this made me very afraid. On 14 September Julia constructed a shelter for her ducks, and let me help her. I considered this very nice of her, but note that later on she became somewhat impatient, so I went off to pick blackberries. When I got back, she was once again very friendly. The entry continues,

> ... Suddenly I see A.E. dead tired, call out "Aunt Evelyn" and run towards her. Everyone is very glad to see her. In the evening we go to a concert... On the way home Seb guesses that I didn't enjoy it very much, which is true, but I don't let on. At night A.E. gives us the things she brought back from London for us. Seb admires my ski outfit more than J.'s. Secretly I am somewhat pleased by that, but not too much so because all day long she has been very nice to me.

My last normal day at "Woodlands" was Sunday, 15 September. While London suffered its first daylight raid, far away from that kind of danger, I encountered a very different one. As so often before, I went by myself for a Sunday walk, and while picking blackberries, came upon an appletree whose fruit, according to Gillian, was not any good. Probably I was making sure that her opinion was justified when suddenly I found myself in the midst of three horses and got very frightened. Apparently nothing at all happened, though the diary does not mention how I managed to escape.

By contrast with all these relatively short entries, my account of the following day is filled with minutiae, not only because so much happened on 16 September, but also because every moment of my last day with the C. family became important and precious.

> What a day! I ate my breakfast as usual, but afterwards when I went to A.E.'s room, I knew that something had happened, because all the others had already been to see her. She said "I have news for you Elisabeth". I looked at her and then asked "What?" "I am sorry, but you have to leave." I gazed at the floor because I did not want to let her see my tears, and read the letter which she pressed into my hands. I didn't understand a single word. I couldn't help myself any longer, I threw myself on her bed and cried as I hope I will never have to cry so again. She was very good to me, she let me cry as long as I needed to and then she comforted me.

Genuinely fond of me, and unwilling to expose me to the dangers of the Atlantic, Aunt Evelyn had bowed to the fears of my parents, fears which she herself did not share. However, she had promised to look after me merely for the time being and to return me to my own family as soon as this would prove feasible, so in good conscience she had to let me go. Quite naturally she assumed that I was looking forward to seeing my parents again and that my tears merely showed that I had grown attached to the C.s and hated leaving all of them. The latter was true enough – despite my problematic relationship with Julia – and of course there was also my constant fear of the unknown, so that I preferred the difficulties I knew to whatever might be looming ahead. However, there were also those other reasons which I could not even express to myself, let alone to anyone else. I could hardly tell Aunt Evelyn that I disliked America and didn't want to go there, for aside from everything else, this would have seemed most ungrateful. Even less was I able to say that I was afraid of my mother, and that the prospect of being reunited with her, without Fräuli as intermediary, filled me with dread. England, on the other hand, not only contained a protective Fräuli figure – namely Seb – but also allowed me to flourish in the security of my beloved school, whose new term was just about to start again. Years later, Aunt Evelyn told me that if she had known how afraid I was of my mother, she would never have let me go. Like most children, however, I found such a betrayal impossible, and hence could not give any reasons for tearfully repeating, "I don't want to go", knowing that this inadequate explanation of my feelings would not allow Aunt Evelyn to help me, though I was grateful for her kind words.

Even if not really comforted, at least I was sufficiently calmed to face the rest of the family and the outside world. The diary entry continues,

Seb was very nice to me, and Gillian and Julia likewise. When she gave me her pullover, she asked, "Do you still hate me?" I don't know what I answered because my head was swimming. She went with me to school. I saw Owaissa, Toots,... and two kitchen maids. All were very nice. I wrote to Brittain and to Lois. I couldn't see anything any more. J. bought me chocolate for the journey, and poor Seb came close to losing her head when she tried to pack all my things. The homely goodbye next door moved me far more than the one at school. [Despite everything, my romanticism still came to the forefront. Our neighbours were simple villagers, seen here in a Wordsworthian light.]
In the afternoon we had to buy a suitcase and a few other things.

I took a little pocket money to buy presents. When we got back home, Seb gave me a note from school, and an invitation for the next day. Brittain and Lois wrote to me, and Brittain's letter helped me. In the evening we had another air raid. When I gave them my little presents, Gillian gave me *Ten-Sixty-Six and All That....* A.E.... gave me a book. Afterwards I looked at it and could not contain my joy. It was *The Oxford Book of English Verse.* I broke into tears again when I said good night to A. Evelyn. I thought that Trude [my big doll] would not be able to accompany me, and so I took her to bed with me. But when Seb came upstairs around midnight to go to sleep, she said that she could make a package out of her. – We were able to establish telephone contact with Mrs. H. [where my brother was], but we could not find out when I had to be where.

Aunt Evelyn had made arrangements for my brother and myself to travel together to the U.S. on the same ship. Because of wartime security, Bloomsbury House, still the headquarters for all refugee children, could not give us detailed instructions in advance. The fact that George was staying in a quite different part of the country and had to be notified – via Aunt Evelyn – complicated the procedure, especially since, owing to the frequent London raids, telephone connections were often disrupted. Until the last moment, I expected George to travel with me, for one of my questions to Aunt Evelyn was "If the ship goes down, must I try to save George?", to which she replied firmly that I had to look after myself first. As matters turned out, our "marching orders" reached me at the very last minute, and all attempts to let Mrs. H. know immediately, failed. I left for London, still hoping that George and I would be reunited there, but afraid that if no message reached him on time, then I would have to travel alone. The diary entry for 17 September recounts the story:

This morning I couldn't eat. Even less so when I heard that I would have to leave for London immediately with A. Evelyn. I trembled the whole time and didn't know what I was doing. At last I went next door again, and her mother gave me Tammie's photograph... I kissed Julia, Gillian and Seb. When we drove away in the car, I saw that Seb was crying. That was too much for me and I broke down. At last we got to London with all the suitcases and went to Sheffield Terrace [the C. house in Kensington]. I felt very queer. We still couldn't reach George by phone. He didn't know that he had to leave today, and he caused me much worry. I couldn't eat lunch at all, it was impossible. We went to Bloomsbury House. I had just said goodbye to Antonia [my former ballet instructor] and a few times I had to hold on tight to A. Evelyn and squeeze her hand.

In Bloomsbury House I sat in a corner, surrounded by suitcases, because A. Evelyn left to find out about everything. By now I was crying the whole time without ceasing. A lot of people stopped and tried to comfort me but they didn't succeed because they didn't understand. There was another air raid alarm and A. Evelyn came back and we went into the shelter.

Years later I learnt that when the alarm went off, I had flatly refused to budge because Aunt Evelyn had told me to wait there for her. After numerous attempts to get me to go into the air raid shelter, someone finally contacted her and she came to collect me. The passers-by who earlier had tried to comfort me probably supposed that I was afraid of the bombs, but quite the contrary was true – by now I was beginning to hope that one of them would blow me up. The entry continues,

After some time she had to leave me with some very nice people. But all the others were awful. They laughed and spoke with forced gaiety and their laughter rang hollow: "Yes, there and there during an air raid there is music the whole night long", and all kinds of stuff about internment and concentration camps. After the All Clear, a rather nice lady gave us tea, and then we went to the train station and A. Evelyn came with me because she was helping. She stayed with me for a long time in the train compartment because I didn't want to let her go. Finally she had to leave and I cried even more. A funny looking girl called Utzi tried to comfort me, and at last I gained enough self control to become quiet.

As long as I had Aunt Evelyn to cling to, I was oblivious of everyone else in the compartment, but she herself showed concern for the other children there; in particular, she spent time reassuring two little Jewish boys who did not have their *tefillin* that God would understand and would listen to their prayers. After she had left, the train began its slow journey towards Liverpool. We were told that if it went any faster, it would present a moving target for enemy bombers. At the speed at which it was crawling along, we were reasonably safe from attack.

We travelled through cities over which planes with bombs were hovering, but I didn't care any more. I wished that I could die. Aunt Evelyn had brought me some pretty good news, namely that George would be able to leave with the next ship, but George wasn't I. We were completely alone in Liverpool, and a slightly older girl had to look after us. We had to go into a shelter, and it was horrible there. Finally, when we could come out again, we found the two ladies who were expecting us. We had to wait a long time for a taxi. I sat on someone's lap, but I could feel that she was very uncomfortable, and so I stood up. However my legs were positioned in such a way that I got the worst pain in them that I had had in a long time. It seemed a very long time until we could finally get out, and to my disgust, it was to an orphanage, where we had to sleep in hard beds. However I was much too tired to mind since it was already two o'clock in the morning.

That night Liverpool had what was considered one of its worst raids so far. The ship on which we were to travel was almost hit, but of that we knew nothing. I still remember the feel of our night shelter, that run-down orphanage from which the children had luckily been evacuated some time previously. When early in the morning we were given weak cocoa out of battered tin mugs, unhappy as I was, I felt pity for those unfortunate orphans who normally slept on these hard cots and had no proper china.

Our early rising was followed by endless red tape until finally we were allowed to board the ship. Some time before doing so, we had to turn in our gas masks, which seemed to confirm the fact that we were really leaving the country. Though I felt strangely vulnerable, suddenly stripped of what had been considered essential to my safety, when this took place is not recorded here. The diary entry for 18 September, my last day on English soil, reads:

> We had to get up at six o'clock in the morning, but I could scarcely eat anything for breakfast. Afterwards we went to some office where we had to go through all the papers and then had to wait until noon until all of us were finished. The room in which we had to wait after our papers had been completed was hot, and it was so full that one could scarcely breathe. Another girl who had pigtails was with me. She was awful. She didn't leave me in peace. She talked and laughed, asked me why I cried, and followed me around. Once again, several people tried to comfort me. Finally when we were all finished and had to go in a bus to another office, we were no longer accompanied, and I felt even more alone. We were there for another two-three hours until we could finally board the ship. I had tea and went to bed and woke up a number of times and cried myself to sleep again.

For better or worse, I was about to embark on a voyage which would lead to a new life. The last entries in the diary describe that journey across the Atlantic.

CHAPTER IX
ACROSS THE ATLANTIC

Our ship, the *H.M.S. Antonia*, which was largely filled with English children who were being evacuated for the duration of the war, left Liverpool on 19 September and landed in Montreal eight days later. The English evacuees were separated from us refugee children, and we had relatively little contact with them.

For the first part of our journey we were accompanied by a convoy, but owing to the scarcity of ships, these had to turn back after a few days, leaving us in mid-Atlantic. I remember clearly how our ship suddenly appeared very small and vulnerable, alone upon the vast, grey seas. Since an encounter with U-boats always remained a distinct possibility, from the very beginning of our journey we were drilled regarding procedures in case of attack. As far as I can recall, we were usually ordered below deck, and hence we saw nothing of whatever might have taken place. Utterly selfish in my misery, I prayed throughout the voyage that the boat would sink, though the diary does not mention this fact. It dwells largely on my companions, most of whom had lived in quite different social circumstances from the ones I had enjoyed. A number of them were practising Jews, while some few who had found refuge with relatives, spoke surprisingly little English. I, on the other hand, could still understand, but scarcely speak, my native tongue. As far as I could see, the majority of my shipmates compared very unfavourably with the children I had known at The Garden School where a certain standard of behaviour was taken for granted.

The diary picks up where I had left off the day before, with an account of our first day at sea.

We sailed today, late in the morning. For a long time I looked towards England and we all blessed England after the Captain had explained the safety precautions to us. [How did we "bless" England? Perhaps all said farewell or else prayed for the safety of the country they were leaving.] Once again I cried a lot and talked with the woman with whom I had talked the day before. Also with an English boy, since there are many English children on the ship. Then I wrote to A. Evelyn and cried a little more. Our cabin is very small and four people have to sleep in it. There isn't any room. The cabin steward and the stewardess are both very nice. The same is true of the oldest of our girls, and of another one who doesn't belong to our group. But the fourth one who sleeps with us is like

Daphne [the girl I had admired at school but had found rather domineering?] I don't feel very much like eating.

On the second day out, 20 September, I was either beginning to feel sea-sick or else, not surprisingly, I was suffering the after-effects of so many violent emotional outbursts.

Today I felt terribly sick and stayed in bed, while the others ran around with the sailors. Naturally I talk to them too, but not in the way these do.

The next day more of us got sea-sick.

I read the books that Gillian and A. Evelyn have given me. Yesterday I couldn't read. All the girls here are very, very stupid and are *"backfishes"* [a somewhat derogatory German term denoting a rather silly girl in her early teens]. Even Daphne doesn't have as much character as the real one [at school]. I have found out that she is Catholic, but that doesn't make any difference. Our laundress is very nice and helps me to wash when I feel sick again. She also helps me in the cabin. Daphne declares that I am only lazy and says that she is *not* going to get sick. Secretly, I am pleased when it happens to her.

By the fourth day out – 22 September – there is no more mention of sea-sickness.

Today I wrote again "home", the word which I now use for A. Evelyn's family. All the girls in my cabin mimic the lady with whom I talked, and other people too, and I have to do the same thing when I am in the cabin, otherwise I wouldn't be a "good sport". I tell them that Julia's book [no other reference] isn't very nice, so that they won't ask to borrow it. Lutzi and Paul quarrelled, and Lutzi hit Paul because he went to the tavern. When she came out, I went inside and talked with Paul. Afterwards I went to have a talk with Lutzi. I told her that one mustn't shout at Paul or hit him, but that one should be nice to him and attempt to gain his trust. For he is really a very nice lad.

Needless to say, I have no recollection of this early attempt at match-making, and would dearly like to know what I said to the beer-drinking Paul and what on earth he made of this earnest child who was suddenly holding him a lecture. Lutzi, one of the girls to whom I felt closest on the whole voyage, was certainly somewhat older than I. My general assessment, that all the girls were *"backfishes"* does not seem to have applied to her. The next day's entry describes a family whose background must have been similar to my own, since I felt immediate sympathy with them.

At the table in the dining-room is a very nice Viennese girl called Susi Weiss. Her parents are very nice too. The whole family is the only one I like. All the others are horrible. Everyone wears a turban [apparently a female fashion on board]. I think that it looks very vulgar. Today I bought myself a scarf and when Daphne wound it around my head, I took it off again immediately. Only Lutzi, with whom I talked, understands why.

My dislike for what I considered vulgar went hand in hand with a Puritan disapproval of teenage flirtations, behaviour which I associated with lower class standards. There was plenty of this to be found on the ship, as the entry for 24 September shows.

I talked a little bit with Daphne today. She thinks that I am somewhat crazy because I told her that I like to get out of bed in the middle of the night and play a role [i.e. pretend to be another person]. She told me confidentially about Elsie who runs around too much with one of the sailors, but I think that she tells this to everyone. And although Daphne pretends otherwise, as far as I can see, she too runs around much too much.

Today I thought that I smelled, but decided that that was nonsense because I had had a bath, but nevertheless the smell remained. A Jew, who thought that I belonged to the Jewish faith, invited me to a religious service on Thursday. Luckily Gina was there and answered for herself, and when I told her that I was Catholic, she promised to tell him if he asked. [Not only was I embarrassed, but also I had been addressed in German and couldn't cope.] I was in the adjoining partition of the room when an evening service started and had difficulty to restrain myself from laughing at the priest. But I do not want to mock other people's religion. The whole thing was only a very, *very* rapid murmuring of Hebrew.

My next entry starts with a great deal of philosophising, so obviously little was happening and I had a great deal of time on my hands.

Each day is, or seems to be, quite ordinary, but in reality something changes every day. Little things, big things, all make a difference. When my neighbour's life appears to me to be so ordinary and dull, while mine is so exciting, I must not forget that his small affairs matter to him as much as mine do to me. Perhaps some new idea, other thoughts, discussions, games or a new chapter in a book, all these things are important and change the ordinary routine of one's life.

Today I wrote home again, and then, when I started reading you dear diary, I started crying because I still want to go back to "Woodlands". A few islands, the first sign of land that we had seen for days, became visible. I went up on deck. Cold, grey and foggy, cliffs and rocks, a small church and one or two houses – I don't know whether I was disappointed or if I was too sad to look at it all properly. In any case, I went down below again right away.

I read for a while, and then a girl asked if I would lend her my book of poetry, and I had to say yes, but I could hardly get to sleep with A. Evelyn's last and most precious present in strange hands. I had also lent Gillian's book to someone whom I didn't even know. I rearranged all my own poems, and when Gina saw them, she thought that they were very good. Even though I knew that she is very stupid, nevertheless I was pleased.

The ladies' salon is now always full of men. It's the spot where all the German and the Jewish men gather, and even though I don't like them, it's interesting. One is like Vati [the usual childish form for father]. Perhaps not as far as his face is concerned, but his bearing and his speech are so like Vats [Apparently an early attempt to find a pet name for my father that would align with my mother's; quite soon, the childish "Vati" became transformed into "Vits".] that I like him very much. Another man is very fond of Lutzi and me and gives us chocolate. He is very nice.

Daphne is terribly stupid. She soaks everyone's bed with water. She made mine wet with beer, and I hate her that much more now.

The entry for 26 September claims that a great deal happened that day, but in a thoroughly self-centred way, the diary is mainly concerned with my own artistic and literary endeavours.

... Late in the evening all of us walked across the deck. The night was very beautiful and we saw the Northern Lights, but the children played so many jokes and silly stuff like that that it was all spoiled. Early in the morning one of the girls gave me my poetry book back and I was very glad. Another girl liked my drawings. I showed some of my own poems to that nice gentleman, and he wanted to discuss "The World" [title of a poem?] with me, but I didn't feel like doing so. In the morning several boys and Daphne prepared an "applepie" bed for Lutzi. We watched her when she went to bed and she was terribly angry even though she didn't let on. In any case, she doesn't want to talk with any of us anymore.

The diary makes no mention of sailing down the St. Lawrence and claims that we landed at "Quebeque". Perhaps I got confused by sailing past the old city, or possibly I remembered from my geography lessons that we would be reaching this province, and was merely showing off. When we finally disembarked at Montreal, the English evacuees stayed in Canada, while most of the refugee children were put on a train going to the United States. All this required endless red tape, which started as soon as we had docked on 27 September.

The lady returned Gillian's book to me, and as far as possible I made friends with Lutzi again. The stewardess told us that we would be getting off the boat early tomorrow morning, and finally I am excited and happy to go to Mama and Vati. I finished my letter to Aunt Evelyn and it got a little more cheerful at the end. It was beautiful on deck. We landed at Quebeque [sic] and saw a few soldiers, etc. I tried the whole time to find out if I liked Quebcck [sic] with the result that I didn't find out anything. In the evening we had to sort out our papers again. I talked for a long time with Susi. But suddenly I lost my head. Luckily Gina was there and she helped me with the packing, and Scottie was able [the entire construction is an English one, and the last word is actually in English] to change a pound note for me which I needed for tips. The man in the office was very nice, but I couldn't go to bed till eleven o'clock, and tomorrow I have to get up at six-thirty. With the passing of time, Lutzi becomes a bit more friendly.

While the entry isn't very explicit as to why I lost my head, I can guess what happened. Presumably we were expected to pack our suitcases that night, but instead of getting on with the job, I chatted with Susi whose parents were looking after her belongings. Then I panicked, overwhelmed at the thought of all that lay ahead. Gina came to my rescue, and was there again when we finally disembarked on 28 September.

Today we were awakened early and after breakfast, from which I saved an orange and two rolls, we gave the waiters their tips. Afterwards we had to go for several hours through more examinations, and therefore did not have time to see Montreal. We were busy with papers until lunch time, then we had to go on land to get our luggage, and everyone was very nice. Finally we got into a bus. Everywhere there were posters and notices in French as well as in English, and the bus conductor spoke French too. I was glad that I knew a little.

We went to a hotel and sat outside on the lawn in the sun. An old woman passed by and spoke to us. She thought that we were very brave and courageous. She said that we would like it here, even if, since we loved England, we would want to go back there after the war. We talked with her for some time, and I think that she believed that we were English. I wish I were. Afterwards we went inside. Susi was very nice and asked me to her table, so Gina was alone.

After supper we fetched our passports and then went to the railway station. Gina stayed with me, and when we stepped into the train, I moved far away from ... [people I obviously wished to avoid]. In the crush I behaved pretty brutally [the construction is

faulty and might equally well mean "I was treated pretty brutally"],
but one can understand that. At long last we all got a seat, but in
our compartment there were five people who kept on laughing so
much that we had no peace. At one point I almost went outside,
but Gina didn't want to come. At last we fell asleep together, holding hands.

I do not recall Gina, whose kindness I seem to have taken very
much for granted in the same way as I underrated her intelligence.
However, I remember that train ride well for we travelled all
night and had to sleep sitting up. Gina put her head in my lap, and
I used her shoulder as my cushion; or perhaps it was the other
way round, but somehow we both managed to sleep fairly soundly
in that rather awkward position. However, when we arrived in
New York City on Sunday, 29 September, there was no one at the
station to meet us.

When we woke up this morning, we had to go and wash in the
First Class. A few ladies were there and they were very nice, so
we chatted a little. We (Gina and I) went to a window where there
was another boy looking out, but the minute that he left, she started
to talk. At last we saw skyscrapers and New York, but nobody
was at the railway station. There were people waiting for everyone
else, and my eyes filled with tears when I saw children with their
parents. At last a lady from the Jewish Committee came and took
Gina and me, and a few others to her office by means of a subway.
There she asked for my name, etc. and inquired if I knew anyone
in New York. I told her about Mrs. Rose, but I didn't have her
address. At last she found the landlady with whom my mother had
lived, and she was supposed to come and get me. I sat there and
waited, chatted a little, looked down into the street and read a
magazine, full of murderers and horrible monsters. Suddenly two
older ladies and a gentleman came to get me. I didn't know them
and I was pretty frightened.

At this point the diary breaks off, and the gaps have to be filled
by memory. That the latter cannot be trusted completely is
evidenced by the fact that I recall myself standing at that huge
railway station, totally alone. Gina and the "few others" are not
there. I suppose that the sheer terror I felt at finding myself
somewhere where I didn't want to be in the first place, and then
on top of that, apparently abandoned, accounts for the blank in
my mind. While this traumatic situation was unfortunate, I was
probably not the only child to whom it happened because, owing
to wartime security, parents could not be notified when, and on
what ship, they might expect their children. Indeed, since these

ships had to zigzag their way across the Atlantic, out-
manoeuvering U-boats, there could have been no fixed date of
arrival. Presumably some communication had been sent from
Montreal to New York, enabling members of the Jewish
Committee for Refugees to be on the alert. Gina and the other
children were quickly identified and picked up because their
relatives lived in New York City and had connections with the
Jewish Committee. I, however, was more difficult to place because
my parents lived in Buffalo, which was over fourhundred miles
away, a considerable distance in those days, and while I knew
their postal address, I could not supply the office with a telephone
number at which they might be reached. The Jewish Committee
had registered my parents when they first arrived from Europe,
but had long ago lost touch with them, especially after my father,
never a practising Jew, had become a devout Catholic. Luckily,
the Committee's dead files still contained the address of the
lodgings which my parents had occupied before leaving for upstate
New York, and after a lengthy search, these were eventually
located. The landlady who remembered my parents knew how to
get in touch with Mrs. Rose. And so two strange ladies,
accompanied by a gentleman, finally appeared to collect me.

If waiting abandoned at the train station had been terrifying,
the woman from the Jewish Committee who collected us waifs
and strays confirmed all my worst anti-U.S. fears and prejudices.
Here was someone who chewed gum incessantly and spoke with an
appalling accent – far worse than Raymond Gram Swing! She
shepherded her charges through the New York subway system,
and the pushing and shoving such travel necessitated convinced
me that America was an unpleasantly violent society – a view which
the magazine she gave me to read did nothing to dispel. It was hardly
an auspicious start to my new life, and I promised myself that
some day I would get back to England; meanwhile, even if I could
not be English, I would keep myself uncontaminated from
American influences in manners and in speech. Numerous teachers
who subsequently tried to flatten my English "a" were exceedingly
puzzled why I failed to comprehend them, but I had already discovered
what a potent weapon passive resistance could be.

My parents' former landlady, a Mrs. Birk, had indeed been
able to contact Mrs. Rose, for along with this dumpy, bustling
figure, there came into the room a stately, aristocratic lady, our
"Aunt Addie", a cultured American *grande dame* who through
marriage had become distantly related to my mother's family. In

my memory she is accompanied by her eldest son, but the last diary entry, which is probably more reliable on this point, claims that the man was Mrs. Birk's brother. Long before I was born, Aunt Addie had frequently visited Vienna, always staying in an elegant hotel on the Ring; widowed and no longer able to travel, she lived permanently in a large suite in one of the older grand hotels off Fifth Avenue. Thanks to her generosity and support, my parents had been able to emigrate to the U.S. at the last minute; coming to the rescue once more, she now offered to accept responsibility for me. After initial explanations and a quick meal, I was sent to stay with the loquacious landlady to await the arrival of my mother. The next two days passed in a blur. I remember being taken to a large apartment and being given some kind of laxative because Mrs. Birk was firmly convinced that starting with a clean slate helped one's stomach to adjust. Later on in the evening a fire siren went off in the vicinity, and instinctively I rushed towards the door, trying to get downstairs. The next day Aunt Addie took me to her bank and explained American coinage to me.

Shortly thereafter my mother arrived, for among my family letters is one which she wrote to my father, which is simply dated "Wednesday". I have no recollection of our first meeting, but according to her pencilled jottings, my mother found me "very grown up and tremendously sensible". She also worried about expenditures because I was always hungry, reporting that for lunch I had no trouble disposing of "a veal chop with two fried eggs, two tomatoes, bread and butter, followed by masses of fruit". We trudged around together in torrents of rain, trying to find out when my brother would be arriving. My mother was suitably impressed by my English gumboots, which in nursery language I still referred to as my "gollyboots", and amused by the curious German I tried to produce for her benefit. As a result, all our conversations had to be carried on in English, though she told my father that my accent was not very good, a fact she attributed to my poor ear. As far as I can recall, after all this time I still couldn't pronounce a proper "th", but it took only a few months in the U.S., where my pronunciation was rarely corrected and where I was not constantly scrutinised, and suddenly I no longer had any trouble with it.

Wartime secrecy was aggravated by the fact that the various committees responsible for refugee children did not necessarily cooperate with one another. Hence my mother was sent from one to another. The Jewish Committee which had collected me told us that two more ships were expected that week, and another agency produced the information that George was already on his way, sponsored by the Catholic Committee. Aware of the difficulties which had confronted me, my mother did not want to subject my brother to a similar experience and therefore decided to await the arrival of these two ships. Explaining the matter to my father, she writes that quite apart from the difference in our ages, I at least had wanted to come to my parents, although I had been very upset at leaving England, whereas George had flatly refused to budge! While there is little evidence to justify either assessment, there is at least a written record describing my brother's state of mind. In a long letter, addressed to Aunt Evelyn, Mrs. H. details how she took my brother to Bloomsbury House, hoping that he could still catch up with me, and when that proved impossible, how she found him suitable accommodations for the night. This letter, as well as some earlier ones, shows her great concern for my brother; interestingly, she is always careful to allow him to keep the German spelling of his name. Mrs. H.'s letter, describing her day in London, mentions some extremely unpleasant air raids that took place while she was at Bloomsbury House and notes that the conditions in the shelter were dreadful and very depressing, confirming my perception of them, as described in the diary. Somewhat ruefully, she admits that when she left my brother in the care of a much older boy who was going to show him the sights, and who was also prepared to look after him the following morning if she herself could not get back to town,

> Georg was delighted. I'd like to be able to tell you *he* wept on parting but I can't. He was so thrilled at his new companion he could hardly wait to say goodbye.

Although Mrs. H. returned to her own family that evening, she came up to London again the following day to make sure that George got off safely, and at that point found quite a different little boy waiting for her. Much later she sent Aunt Evelyn a postcard, recounting that she too had had a cable announcing his safe arrival in the U.S., and telling her,

> I'm so utterly thankful. I went up to see Georg again and found a very strained looking pathetic lad. Could hardly forbear bringing him back and not letting him go after all. But we're by no means too good here...

While the H. family were concerned about George's safety on

their side of the Atlantic, my mother was even more worried on the other. Hence, despite the expense involved in staying on in New York – and my mother's letter is filled with money worries – we waited... and waited. At last came the grim news that a ship had been lost at sea with all the children on board, though I am not sure that at the time I myself was told of this disaster. My mother, who had no way of knowing whether it was the one on which my brother had been placed, though frantic with fear, continued to hope. A day or so later the third ship arrived safely, and when we went to meet the train, there was my brother, unscathed. Grimy from head to foot, he had spent the whole train journey in the engine room, and was still so exuberant from this experience, that little else mattered to him. His crossing had been quite different from mine. Whereas the passengers of the *H.M.S. Antonia* had been ordered below whenever the possibility of danger loomed, and were not certain that they had really encountered any, George reported watching on deck as planes were being shot down. The thrilling adventures through which he had lived seemed to compensate him for having had to leave England. Nor did he ever attempt to maintain contact with the family which had looked after him so long, probably because he had preferred his first home in the North, and still resented the exchange. Quite soon, he adopted an American accent.

POSTSCRIPT

The appalling loss of so many young lives to German U-boats made everyone reassess the situation. As might be expected, the ship on which my brother crossed the Atlantic was the last to sail on such a mission. Had Aunt Evelyn not moved heaven and earth to reunite us with our parents as quickly as possible, we might have been forced to spend the war years in England. Whether or not that would have been preferable, I cannot judge today, though no doubt, had I had any real choice in the matter, I would have wanted to stay. In that case, I would certainly have received a far better educational grounding than the one which American parochial and state schools provided, but might have suffered in other ways. One cannot build one's life on "ifs". Ultimately, the experiences with which fate presents us, rather than the ones we would have liked to choose for ourselves, become part of the stuff of what we are; if one does not want to disintegrate completely, one has to come to terms with that.

This account began with a little silver cross and a very large doll named Trude. Though I had treasured the little cross, symbol of my faith, now that I could attend church again regularly, I hardly noticed when and where I lost the pendant. It had been a parting gift from the father I loved, but since he himself was back in my life, it no longer had the same sentimental value. Trude, symbol of my childhood, soon disappeared as I became overwhelmed by adolescence, poverty, and the strain under which my parents, and especially my mother, were living. The sympathetic understanding between us, established in those first few days in New York, did not endure, and the next six years were perhaps the most unhappy ones of my whole life. The dream of escape, of returning to England, cast a golden glow over the time I had spent there. Aunt Evelyn's wartime letters, with their continued encouragement and moral support, unintentionally re-enforced such a view. So did that love of English literature which I shared with her.

My childhood diary corrects any idealised picture and presents a far more realistic one, even if much of what it says shows limited insight. Surprisingly, despite still looking back with longing, I was already attempting an assessment of my stay in England soon after settling in the States. This last diary entry is in English, written in Buffalo, N.Y. on 3 July 1941, when I am almost fourteen years old. Unfortunately, it breaks off abruptly, probably owing to lack of privacy. When presenting it here with all its errors in grammar and spelling, I must stress that it too cannot be taken as the absolute truth, since the diarist who attempts "to analyse the situation calmly" is a profoundly unhappy adolescent desperately seeking an explanation for at least some of her current miseries:

> I've forgotten all my German dear diary, I haven't had time to write till now, and besides I'm in a temper, in trouble...
>
> When I first arrived in New York I was fetched by Mrs. Birk, her brother and by Mrs. Addie Rose. I was rather frightened because they looked so strange. I remember the same feeling when I first met Aunt Evelyn. I believe that it was then created by her red lipstick and the hat she wore. So if I felt funny then, you can imagine what I felt like now. Besides in '39 I wanted to go to England; in '40 I did not want to go to America.
>
> Now let us try calmly to analyse the situation. There was I, a young girl of not quite 13 [I celebrated my thirteenth birthday less than two months after arriving in the States], leaving a country in which I had lived nearly two years and which I truly loved, even if I did not care for, or hated a great many of its people. In addition to that, I was going to a country towards which I was allready [sic] strongly prejudiced, and I was going to meet my parents again, parents to which [sic] I was attached, but in whose midst I had always felt lost and in my childhood I remember that I turned instead to my dear governess "Fräuli". I had not forgotten her, but time had dampened my affectiones [sic] for her allready [sic] and besides *she* was not going to meet me here.
>
> In addition to all this I had all my living friends, and by this phrase I mean those friends whom I loved because they were among me and not because I had once loved them and only remembered that, I had left all my friends behind and had just finished the most trying time of my life – the time I spent on the ship the H.M.S. ANTONIA. Now that I had really left England, or rather the few days that I knew that I was leaving, I had felt myself bound closer to all in England than ever before in my life. The reason was a very simple one – I had no one else to turn to. At that moment I put every other passion aside and only felt a great loving for them all – even Julia.
>
> I had learned a great deal in England, first and foremost I had learned English but I had also learned some Latin and had developed my French. I had been taught more graceful movements, better manners and several other subjects. But I had also been ridiculed and hated and that has left a strong impression on my mind. To this day, six months later and I believe that it will be for allways [sic], I have been afraid of humans. I don't want to admit

it, but it is true. In my mind I always feel "they don't like me, there is something wrong with me". At the most difficult stage of our growth I was being constantly criticized and I still feel constantly that everyone "weighes" me, and I am afraid. At school, in the street, in church, at home, even when I play with children of only five or six I have that feeling and I cannot conquer it. That was one of the defects of my education... Nevertheless...

Who knows what that "nevertheless" would have included? I am glad that at the end, the "great loving" wiped out so much of the supposed hate, for I am sure that there never was any directed towards me – impatience, frustration and intermittent, understandable jealousy perhaps, but nothing worse. On my part too, the response of "I hate" which turns up repeatedly in the diary, merely indicated temporary dislike. However, children deal in absolutes, and hence I could only express strong emotions in black and white terms. Undoubtedly too much criticism, even though well intentioned, came my way, and the awareness that this did me considerable harm is quite correct. However the power to do damage lay further back than I realised at the time. Ridicule? Solemn and self-conscious as a child, I had difficulty distinguishing between jest and earnest. It took at least thirty years of living and a great deal of bawdy mediaeval literature to develop a sense of humour in me!

It took me even longer to accept who I was. For my desire to be English, which had surfaced during our brief conversation with the old woman in Montreal, represented more than just longing for the chance to return to England after the war. On a far deeper level, it expressed profound dissatisfaction with who and what I was. Writing in the forties, Nancy Mitford wittily pinpointed the blimpish Englishman who is convinced that "Abroad is bloody and foreigners are fiends". Miss Mitford's description entails only a slight exaggeration, for this serene assumption of effortless superiority was still very real, especially among the upper middle classes. With all my heart and soul I accepted this stance, whereas other foreigners were more critical. In *How To Be An Alien*, George Mikes, the talented Hungarian author and cartoonist, neatly satirised the contemporary British attitude towards all Central Europeans, including the many refugees seeking asylum in England at the time. Yet although I knew this little book well, and could even laugh at its jokes, I still hoped that my acceptance into an English family and my English schooling would somehow, miraculously, transform me. The realisation that I would always remain a foreigner in the land I loved only came many years later, when I was already an adult. At the time that I wrote my last entry in the diary, I was still struggling with numerous selves that needed to be sorted out – the Austrian refugee who wanted to pass as English, the Jew who wasn't a Jew but a Catholic, the upper middle class girl reduced to living in what was practically a slum tenement, the child who rejected the claims of blood and preferred a distant foster-mother... It would be a long time before all these different selves could be reconciled in some measure, allowing me to become a whole person. My childhood years in England were only partially responsible for all these difficulties of course, but their influence had been a profound one. Ultimately, force of circumstances rather than deliberate choice enabled me to discover what had been positive in them, and to integrate that into the unfolding pattern of my life. Or, to express it differently and in keeping with a Portuguese proverb, God managed to write straight with crooked lines. Happy are those who at the close of day no longer wish to alter a single line!

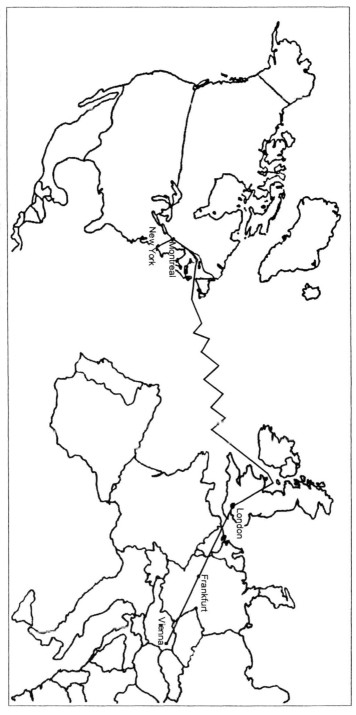

Map showing Elisabeth's gradual journey from Vienna to New York.

CATHOLIC COMMITTEE FOR REFUGEES FROM GERMANY

EDUCATION BRANCH

HON SECRETARY
Mr. J.V.A. Reid.

Telephone:
WESTERN 8487

Office :
C.C.I.R.
KENSINGTON PALACE MANSIONS
DE VERE GARDENS
LONDON, W.8

Mrs.   C
London, W.8.

Dear Mrs. C

        Thank you very much for letting us know that Georg
Ornstein will be leaving Penrith and going to a guaranteed
home found for him by the Inter Aid Committee.   It is very
kind of you to put him up for two night-s in London and we
are sure that Georg and Elisabeth will be very pleased to
see each other again.
        With renewed thanks for all your kindness,

                                Yours sincerely,

                                J.V.A. Reid

                                Hon. Secretary.

Letter acknowledging George's move from Penrith.

REFUGEE CHILDREN'S MOVEMENT, LTD.

BLOOMSBURY HOUSE, BLOOMSBURY STREET, LONDON, W.C.I

26-8-40   Telephone : MUSeum 2900   Ex: 69

We have obtained your American
Visa to-day, so there will be no
need for you to come to the
Consulate again.

        for Mrs Lorna Phipps

                                A.T.

Confirmation of Elisabeth's American Visa.

OXFORD REFUGEE COMMITTEE

Patrons : The Right Worshipful The Mayor.
The Vice-Chancellor.

Bankers :
Glyn Mills & Co., Oxford.

Interviewing Hours :
Mon. & Tues., 3—4 p.m.
Wed. & Sat., 11—12 (noon).
Thurs., 3—5 p.m.

All communications to be addressed to
the Secretary.

29 NEW-INN-HALL STREET,
OXFORD.

CHILDREN'S SUBCOMMITTEE

Telephone ▓▓▓▓
47302

Jan. 27, 1939

Dear Madam,

I think you have been in communication with Mr Espir about the
boy Georg Ornstein, who I understand is now in England under the
charge of your committee.   A Mrs D   of W   Manor,

C   , Oxon. has been interested in him through seeing his ▓▓▓
case papers, and would, I think, be willing to take him and see
him through his education if some help or backing were forthcoming
I understood from Mr Espir that he was at present settled very far
from his sister, and that it might be better if he could be finally
settled somewhere in the south.   Mrs D   has written to me:

His being a Catholic is by no means a handicap, in fact quite the
reverse, and we have a small chapel and visiting Jesuit Father
attending it. I would be grateful if you would put me into touch
with the Catholic Refugee Committee. If there was the possibility
that they might arrange for his education in a Catholic school that
would make a great difference to us. We ourselves are Church of
England but should be most particular about a child attending his
own church.

Mrs D   has a small daughter of about 9 and two sons of
17 and 19. Her husband is retired and not in strong health, but I
understand they are comfortably off and the boy would have a very
pleasant home. She is anxious for him to be of 'gentle birth' as
being a good deal with her child, but I gather Georg fulfills this
Perhaps you would communicate with her direct? She will keep me
informed.

Yours truly
Geonnne Bailey Hon Ref Registrar

Letter to Mrs C. noting that George has been offered a home nearer Elisabeth.